DURKHEIM

Is

Dead!

DURKHEIM Is Dead!

Sherlock Holmes
Is Introduced to
Sociological Theory

Arthur Asa Berger

ALTAMIRA
PRESS

A Division of
ROWMAN & LITTLEFIELD PUBLISHERS, INC.
Walnut Creek • Lanham • New York • Oxford

ALTAMIRA PRESS
A Division of Rowman & Littlefield Publishers, Inc.
A Member of the Rowman & Littlefield Publishing Group
1630 North Main Street, #367
Walnut Creek, CA 94596
www.altamirapress.com

Rowman & Littlefield Publishers, Inc.
A Member of the Rowman & Littlefield Publishing Group
4501 Forbes Boulevard, Suite 200
Lanham, MD 20706

PO Box 317
Oxford
OX2 9RU, UK

Copyright © 2003 by ALTAMIRA PRESS

Illustrations by Arthur Asa Berger

British Library Cataloguing in Publication Information Available

Library of Congress Cataloging-in-Publication Data

Berger, Arthur Asa, 1933–
   Durkheim is dead! : Sherlock Holmes is introduced to sociological
theory / Arthur Asa Berger.
     p. cm.
   Includes bibliographical references and index.
   ISBN 0-7591-0299-6 (cloth : alk.paper)—ISBN 0-7591-0300-3 (pbk. : alk. paper)
   1. Holmes Sherlock (Fictitious character)—Fiction. 2. Watson, John H. (Fictitious
character)—Fiction. 3. Private investigators—England—Fiction. 4. Sociology—
Fiction. I. Title.

PS3602.E753 D87 2003
813'.54—dc21

                                 2002151885

Printed in the United States of America

table of **contents**

author's **note**

Durkheim is Dead! is a mystery novel. It features the great consulting detective Sherlock Holmes and his trusted companion, Dr. John Watson. But it is also, like many mysteries, a novel of ideas and the ideas in this story are those of some of the most important sociologists and social thinkers of the nineteenth and twentieth centuries (in alphabetical order): W. E. B. Du Bois, Emile Durkheim, Sigmund Freud, Vladimir Lenin, Georg Simmel, Beatrice Webb, and Max Weber.

I've had a great deal of fun writing it and I hope you will find this little mystery novel both entertaining and edifying. It is not an easy thing, believe me, to make sociological theory, written at the turn of the twentieth century, palatable, let alone digestible in the twenty-first. On the other hand, there is something inherently fascinating and interesting about sociological theory, which attempts to explain why people behave the way they do. So I hope you come away from reading this book with an appreciation both of the formidable powers of intellect the various characters in the story have and of the insights they have provided about that most curious of matters—the social behavior of human beings.

You will learn about bureaucracies, normless (anomic) behavior, suicide, the relation between religion and capitalism, the
different kinds of authority, charisma, class conflict, the unconscious, the Oedipus Complex, feminist ideas, the power of beliefs
and values, problems relating to race, the power of collective representations, symbols, and many other matters in this book.

I have cast a wide net, and included some thinkers who
may be a bit peripheral to traditional courses on sociological theory. But I wanted to deal with feminist thought (which is why
Beatrice Webb is in the book), with Freudian thought (he does
have some interesting ideas about the psyche and social phenomena that are worth considering), and with Marxist thought (in the
person of Lenin, since Marx died well before the events in this
novel took place). I also had to tell a story that dealt with sociological theory, and that created certain problems for me as far as de-
termining who would be in the story and why they did what they
did.

As a result of reading this book, which deals with a fascinating and important subject—sociological theory—you might
even find out where some of your ideas about your place in the
scheme of things and your notions about your possibilities come
from.

I have used some important passages from material written
by my theorists and others as dialogue in certain places in this
book to capture their ideas as accurately as possible and give read-
ers a sense of their style of writing. That explains the antiquated or
awkward nature of the language in some of the passages. It has
been necessary to make some changes, here and there, in these
passages to make them more readable.

I have also made use of material found in Lewis Coser's
classic *Masters of Sociological Thought*, Hendrik M. Ruitenbeek's *Varieties of Classic Social Theory*, and Peter and Brigitte Berger's *Sociology: A Biographical Approach*, and others, as well as the works of

the social theorists dealt with in the book. I want to express my appreciation to the reviewers of my book when it was in manuscript form. I don't know who they were, but they made a number of very useful suggestions. I have also drawn a number of illustrations to make the book more visually attractive and provided a glossary of important terms at the end of the book.

[*Note:* In this text I use the term "Negro" for historical accuracy, since that was the term conventionally used at the time of the story. I also use terms like "man's progress" for human progress and discuss matters like women getting the right to vote instead of more contemporary issues such as equality in the home, community, and workplace in the interest of verisimilitude.]

acknowl**edgments**

This book, like a number of other books I have written, grew out of a conversation I had with Mitch Allen, president of AltaMira Press, at a Chinese restaurant. I mentioned that I was relieved that my comic mystery, *The Mass Comm Murders: Five Media Theorists Self-Destruct,* was finally going into production. I had originally given my manuscript for *The Mass Comm Murders* to him, but because he doesn't publish books on mass communications, he sent it on to Brenda Hadenfeldt, an editor at Rowman & Littlefield Publishers, with whom I did a book on advertising. AltaMira Press, I should add, is a part of Rowman & Littlefield.

Then I said to Mitch, "I'm thinking of trying my hand at another murder mystery—I was thinking of writing an introduction to sociology."

"No," he said, "You don't want to write a mystery about sociology . . . but one about social theory. To go with your mystery about postmodern theory, *Postmortem for a Postmodernist* [which he was courageous enough to publish], and your mystery on communication theory. Do another theory book!"

"I take it you're talking about the classic social theorists," I said. "Marx, Weber, Simmel, Durkheim, Freud . . . is that what you had in mind?"

"Yes," he said. "We should also have something on feminism and on race relations."

"Hmm," I thought. "Why not!"

That's because Mitch, whom I have with good reason called "The Great Rejecter," has in the past only published books of mine that *he* suggested I write.

"I've got a title," I said. "*Durkheim Is Dead!* How does that strike you?" I like alliterative titles for my mysteries. My other two mysteries are called *Postmortem for a Postmodernist* and *The Mass Comm Murders.*

"That's it," he said. "That's it. *Durkheim Is Dead!* Let's make it a Sherlock Holmes mystery, too," he added.

All my other mysteries had Inspector Solomon Hunter of the San Francisco Police as the lead detective. And I was thinking of using him again, but since Mitch wanted a Sherlock Holmes mystery, a Sherlock Holmes mystery was what he'd get. Besides, I thought it would be a lot of fun to try my hand at a Sherlock Holmes mystery.

It so happens, in an earlier incarnation, I had read a considerable amount of social theory and had a number of books by social theorists in my library. I also found other books in the San Francisco State University library and the Mill Valley library. The glossary is similar to one I wrote for my book *Media and Communication Research Methods* (Sage) but is considerably modified.

It turns out that around 1910, Max Weber, Sigmund Freud, Vladimir Lenin, Georg Simmel, Emile Durkheim, Beatrice Webb, and W. E. B. Du Bois—the lead characters in this mystery—were all alive and at the height of their intellectual powers. That year, we find:

W. E. B. Du Bois (1868 to 1963) was forty-two

Emile Durkheim (1858 to 1917) was fifty-two

Sigmund Freud (1856 to 1939) was fifty-four

Vladimir Lenin (1870 to 1924) was forty

Georg Simmel (1858 to 1918) was fifty-two

Beatrice Webb (1858 to 1943) was fifty-two

Max Weber (1864 to 1920) was forty-six

It is entirely possible that, in the course of their long careers, they had all met one another and it is conceivable that they all could have met at a conference in London, where this story takes place. (In reading the proto-feminist social activist and writer Beatrice Webb's journal, it would seem that she met just about everyone of consequence who ever set foot in or near London.)

Whether they all had the pleasure of making the acquaintance of the great consulting detective Sherlock Holmes and his associate Dr. Watson, before the events I have described in this tale, is a matter for pure conjecture.

pers**onae**

Sherlock Holmes . . . the most famous consulting detective of all time, Holmes is famous for solving some incredibly baffling crimes due to his remarkable powers of observation and logical analysis. He can also be aloof and imperious. Among his most important cases are *A Study in Scarlet, The Hound of the Baskervilles,* and *The Sign of Four.* In addition to his intelligence, Holmes is a talented musician who plays the violin beautifully. Holmes's intellectual brilliance and ability to make astonishing deductions are put to the test, as he becomes caught in a tangled web of events involving some social thinkers who came to London to give lectures in an international conference on "The Promise of Social Progress."

Dr. John Watson . . . Holmes's good friend and associate, who was a partner in Holmes's greatest cases. Holmes often makes incredible demands on Watson's time, which he accepts in his typically good-natured manner. Watson's knowledge of medicine and his trusty revolver are often put to use in the cases on which Holmes works. It is Watson who recounts Holmes's many adventures, showing Holmes's prodigious intellect in action. Watson also, it turns out, has an interesting theory about the nature of criminality and its relation to biological and neurological phenomena.

Max Weber (1864–1920) . . . professor of sociology at the most prestigious German universities and a thinker of international reputation. His work on "ideal types," the relation between Protestant asceticism and capitalism, and scientific methodology is known to all in his field, as are his theories about the role of bureaucracies in society and the different types of authority that exist in societies and how these types of authority evolve.

Weber is a troubled man who had a nervous breakdown in 1897 and suffered from depression for a number of years. Over the course of time, however, he recovered to some degree and went on to write *The Protestant Ethic and the Spirit of Capitalism* and various other works on social scientific methodology, among other things.

Marianne Weber (1870–1954) . . . Weber's wife, the former Marianne Schnitger, married Weber in 1893 when she was twenty-two years old. Her husband is one of the most important sociological theorists, but she is also well known as a feminist thinker. Among her books are *Authority and Autonomy in Marriage, Woman and Objective Culture,* and *The New Woman.* She received an honorary doctorate from Heidelberg University for her contributions to scholarship about women.

Emile Durkheim (1858–1917) . . . one of the greatest social theorists of the day. He is known for his masterpiece *The Elementary Forms of the Religious Life,* which distinguishes between two realms—the sacred and the profane—and for his theories about anomie or normlessness, deviance, and suicide. He argues that anomie is a reflection of the social structure in which individuals find themselves and not just a state of mind. Durkheim also shows that societies where people were well integrated had lower rates of suicide than those in which people felt alienated and normless. Durkheim is generally thought to be the first French sociologist and the founder of empirical social science.

Georg Simmel (1858–1918) . . . a good friend of Max Weber and an original and highly influential German sociologist whose work on cultural phenomena, on social interactions, on fashion and leisure, and on space and time, attract much attention in the scholarly world. He stresses the importance of interactions among individuals who are continually involved with one another, and the relationship between individuals and groups. Society, he said, is "the name for a number of individuals, connected by interaction." Weber tried, with no success, to obtain a university professorship for Simmel, which he richly deserved. Weber was unable to do so because Simmel was Jewish and the victim of anti-Semitism, which pervaded the German universities of the time.

Vladimir Lenin (1870–1924) . . . whose real name was Vladimir Ilyich Ulyanov, is an important Communist theorist and political figure, who believed in class conflict and the need for a violent revolution. In his theoretical work, he revised classical Marxist ideas that the Communist Revolution would necessarily take place in highly industrialized societies. He suggested that this revolution could take place in economically backward countries and said that Russia was a good candidate for a revolution. Lenin argues that after the Communist Revolution there will be the need for a communist elite to seize power and establish a "dictatorship of the proletariat" to ensure that the revolution is a success. He also stresses the role of imperialism, suggesting that capitalist countries export their problems and exploit underdeveloped countries.

Sigmund Freud (1856–1939) . . . a physician and the originator of psychoanalytic theory, has had a lasting impact on social and political thought. Freud argued that the human psyche has an unconscious that is not accessible to people under ordinary circumstances, which is important because it shapes our behavior. He also divided the psyche into three parts: an id, which is used to described our drives and impulses; an ego, which we use to monitor our surroundings; and a superego, which is similar to conscience. As Freud put it, "where there is id, let there be ego." Freud was interested in individual psychology but also in group psychology, and used psychoanalytic theory to explain the social as well as the individual behavior of people. He dealt with social phenomena in books such as *Civilization and Its Discontents* and *Group Psychology and the Analysis of the Ego.*

W. E. B. Du Bois (1868–1963) . . . an internationally known figure and one of the most influential black scholars of his day. In 1895, he was the first African American to receive a Ph.D. from Harvard, writing his dissertation on the suppression of the slave trade to Africa. Du Bois argued that class and social structure were the basic reasons for social conflict. He also suggested racism was the central problem of the day, an unconventional idea for people of the time. "The problem of the twentieth century is the problem of the color line," Du Bois said. The idea struck people as radical, but the passing of time has shown that if racial conflict isn't the only problem we now face, it most certainly is one of the most important ones.

Beatrice Webb (1858–1943) . . . a social activist who was married to Sidney Webb, a famous political figure and social activist. They were among the most important of the non-Marxist socialists, who argued that poverty in modern, industrialist societies was based on the private ownership of the means of production and the desire to maximize profits, at the expense of the working classes. She collaborated with her husband on many books and projects dealing with social problems such as poverty and crime. Beatrice and Sidney Webb were founders of the London School of Economics. At one time, she had opposed giving the vote to women, but then she changed her mind, and in her later years she became known as a champion of women's causes.

Lady Cecily Bracknell . . . she inherited a great deal of money from her late husband, Lord Ernest Bracknell, a wealthy industrialist, and used it to set up and run a foundation devoted to helping the poor and other worthy causes. Lady Bracknell was also a good friend of Beatrice Webb, who invited her to a dinner party of social theorists, a number of whom, it turns out, had applied for funds from the foundation she ran.

Egoistic suicide arises from the fact that men no longer see any reason for staying alive; altruistic suicide from the fact that this reason seems to them to lie outside life itself; the third type of suicide, the existence of which we have just established, arises from the fact that their actions become ruleless and that they suffer from this condition. Because of its origin, we shall give to this last species the name anomic suicide.

Assuredly, anomic and egoistic suicide are not without kinship resemblance. Both result from the fact that society is not sufficiently strongly present to the individuals concerned. But the sphere from which it is absent is not the same in both. In egoistic suicide, it is from specifically collective activity that [the claims of and regard for] society are absent, thus leaving such activity destitute of both object and meaning. . . . Despite their similarity, these two types of suicide remain distinct from one another. . . . Furthermore, these two types of suicide do not recruit their clientele from the same social milieus: the one is found primarily in the intellectual occupations, the world of thought, the other in the world of industry and commerce.

Emile Durkheim,
"Society and Anomie."
Quoted in Hendrik M.
Ruitenbeek, ed.
*Varieties of Classic
Social Theory* (335).

chapter **one**

I had seen a patient early that afternoon

and as I found myself in the vicinity of the apartment of my dear friend Sherlock Holmes, on Baker Street, I decided to pay him a visit. I wanted to wish him a happy new year, since that date was just a few days distant. I found Holmes sitting in his velvet arm-chair, with a large stack of newspapers beside him on a small table. He looked surprisingly well. I surmised, from his unusual interest in the newspapers, that he was investigating something. He was smoking a cigarette, as was his custom when he had something weighty on his mind.

"Welcome, my good Watson," he said. He seemed in re-markably good spirits. I noticed that his violin was on a table near him. He had been playing it recently, no doubt. I lacked Holmes's formidable powers of observation and analysis, but that wasn't difficult for me to discern. I was relieved that there were no hypodermic needles or other drug paraphernalia to be seen. A good sign.

"I came to wish you a happy new year," I said.

"Thank you, my dear Watson," he replied. "It's good to see you. Since your marriage, I haven't had the pleasure of your company as much as I might desire. So every visit is an occasion of great happiness for me."

"I don't want to keep you from you work," I said. "I see you have a number of newspapers you've been reading."

"You can get a great deal of information from newspapers," Holmes said, "if you read them intelligently. Sometimes they are very useful, even if most of the time they are full of trash."

"Do you have a new case?" I asked.

"I believe so," he said. "I've been contacted by someone about a most delicate matter."

"That is often so," I replied.

"Here," he offered, holding out a small, light blue piece of paper in his hand, "read this."

I took the piece of paper, which was a letter, written in a delicate hand, and read it.

Dear Mr. Holmes:

You are my only hope. I fear that my husband, an eminent sociologist, who has been very troubled in recent years, may commit something violent, and, because he has made a number of enemies, as the result of his lingering mental problems, may the victim of some violence become. He has received threats. I will take the liberty of coming to see you as soon as I am able without fear of being discovered.

M. W.

"Well, what do you make of it, Watson?" asked Holmes. "You know my methods. Try using them."

"I really don't know . . . this woman is terribly fearful . . . she's afraid that her husband may do something terrible to someone . . . I gather he's unstable . . . and he also may be the victim of one of his enemies. Seems like a matter that will require incredible tact," I said. "That's why she wrote you that letter."

"It was delivered by a messenger this morning," Holmes hinted.

"So you have no stamp or postmark to tell you where it was sent from," I replied.

"It was sent from London," Holmes said. "Of that I am fairly certain. People only use messengers within London. The paper is not English. It has a light watermark from a German stationer—an ornate 'B' that is the trademark of a very famous stationer in Berlin, namely the house of Blumenkohl. The paper is of excellent quality, which suggests the woman is married to a person of considerable economic means. But it is slightly faded, and this indicates that the paper is old and that the financial situation of the woman who wrote the note and her husband may be questionable. Also, the construction of the letter, with the verb placed awkwardly at the end of a sentence, tells me that the writer is a native speaker of German and that English is a second or perhaps even third language. The fact that the writer signed her name as 'M. W.' suggests she is anxious and wants to make sure, as best she can, that nobody knows or will be able to find out that she will be using my services or has been using my services, should, somehow, the contents of the letter become public. Of that, my good Watson, she has no reason to fear. And the fact that she has not appeared, yet, despite the urgency of her message Watson, tells me she is anxious and fearful."

"Do you think it is possible that she might not appear?" I asked.

"Not at all," said Holmes confidently. "In fact, I believe she will be sitting in this room within ten minutes."

"Then I'll be off," I said. "I don't wish to interfere with your case."

"No, Watson, you must stay. Your expertise might well be of great use to me in this case. And now, if you will be kind enough to look out from the window overlooking Baker Street and tell me what you see."

I walked over to the window and looked out between the blinds. Across the street from Holmes's residence, 221B Baker Street, I saw a woman, handsomely dressed in a dark blue dress, with a hat and a light veil, glancing at the window of Holmes's apartment. She was fingering her pocketbook nervously.

"There's a woman," I said. "She's glancing at your window from time to time and nervously fingering her pocketbook."

"I think she's just about decided to come," he said. "She was there thirty minutes earlier, trying, no doubt, to summon up enough willpower to see me. She is about to reach the point where she will throw caution to the wind and hazard a visit with me."

Several minutes after Holmes spoke those words, there was a light knock on the door. I walked over and opened it and the woman in the blue dress was standing there.

"May I come in?" she asked.

"By all means," I replied.

"You must excuse me, Mr. Holmes," she said to me, in a slight German accent. Through her light veil I could discern that she had a pained expression on her face. "I desperately need your assistance."

"My name is Watson," I replied. I turned and pointed to Sherlock Holmes, who had come over to greet the woman. "This is the man you are looking for, my dear friend Sherlock Holmes."

"Forgive me," she said, taking off her hat. "I am not from England and only know of the great Sherlock Holmes by his reputation."

She looked like she might collapse at any moment. Her face was blanched and she was trembling slightly.

"Won't you please sit down, Mrs. Weber," said Holmes, motioning the woman to sit on his sofa.

"Thank you," she said, weakly, and sat down. Holmes sat beside her.

"I'm afraid . . . I fear that I may faint."

"Would you like some tea?" he asked. "I can have my housekeeper make some."

"No . . . no thank you," she said. "I don't have a great deal of time."

"I understand," said Holmes.

When she had gathered her strength and composed herself she turned to Holmes.

"But how did you know my name?" she asked.

"The newspapers have had a number of articles about the forthcoming conference titled 'The Promise of Social Progress' and have had articles about the important scholars who will be attending. It not only listed them but it also gave the names of their wives. Your letter paper had a German watermark and you signed it 'M. W.' I had no doubt then that you are, in fact, Marianne Weber, the wife of Professor Max Weber. I have read some of your husband's writings with great interest, and I have read good things about your work on feminist thought, as well."

"My husband," she moaned, and then started weeping.

"Have no fear, Mrs. Weber. I will help you. But you must tell me more."

"My husband," she said, "has had serious psychological problems for many years. A number of years ago, we took a summer trip to Spain. It was a few months or so after my husband had a terrible fight with his father, who died several weeks after their fight. Max always felt he bore a great deal of responsibility for his father's death. When we returned from Spain, Max suddenly became feverish and his fever lasted for more than a month. It finally eased. He then fell into a deep depression and shortly after that had a nervous breakdown. He's never really recovered, though he has been much better for the last five or six years. He's a terribly sad man, Mr. Holmes. Terribly sad. The extent of his illness has not been generally known, I should add. We've tried to keep it a secret as much as possible. He cannot teach but has an arrangement with his university, which has been most generous and which has been supporting him, waiting for the time when he can return to academic life. But I'm afraid this support may be diminished or even terminated. We are managing by making certain economies, but if something happens to him and he cannot return to teaching, I don't know what will happen to us."

"He continues to do some writing and a little bit of teaching, but he is a changed man. He cannot seem to break completely free from his depression, from this terrible sadness that grips him and will not release him. He is able to function to some degree, but he is still ill."

"I understand," said Holmes.

"We're here, along with many other sociologists and social thinkers, for the conference on 'The Promise of Social Progress.' But that is only one reason for our attending the conference. The more important reason is that Max has arranged to see if he can be helped by Sigmund Freud, who is also here for the conference as one of the featured speakers. Freud has agreed to see my husband. They are to meet, discreetly, at a party being thrown for some of the luminaries tomorrow evening. The French sociologist Emile Durkheim will be there and so will Georg Simmel, an old friend of Max. There will be others as well. The Russian political writer Lenin and the Negro social thinker Du Bois, among others. I'm afraid of what Max might do if he has a relapse or what someone might do to him. In Germany we have received some threats. My husband is very outspoken and has offended many people. He's capable of violence, I fear . . . against others and also against himself. I'm terribly scared."

"Mrs. Weber," I reassured her, "you've come to the right man. If anyone can help you, it is Sherlock Holmes. Rest assured, you're in good hands."

"Have you, by chance, notified the police in Germany? Or London?" asked Holmes.

"I was afraid to," she replied. "I'm doing all I can to keep my poor husband's problems secret. It might destroy his career and, even worse, destroy him, if his problems were widely known."

"Yes, yes, I understand," said Holmes. "If you will be kind enough to give me the name of the woman who will be having the party and the details about when and where it will be held, it would be of great help to me."

"The woman is Beatrice Webb and the party will be at Claridge's Hotel at 8:00 P.M. tomorrow evening."

"Beatrice Webb, the feminist thinker," reflected Holmes. "She is a woman of great beauty and profound intellect. I've admired her work and that of her husband Sidney, as well, for many years."

"There will be, I understand, about fifty people at the party," added Marianne Weber. "The conference will be held at

Claridge's Hotel as well. The major lectures by the featured speakers will be held in its main ballroom."

"That is all I need to know," said Holmes. "I've been reading the newspapers carefully from the time I received your letter. This conference has attracted a considerable amount of attention in the press. It has brought writers and thinkers of great prominence from all over the world to London, and the papers are full of articles about these thinkers and their ideas. And photographs of them as well. This new science of sociology seems full of promise, but people are confused by the numerous disagreements these thinkers have with one another. The conference is to last five days. Perhaps, at the end of that period, we will know more about the possibilities for social progress and some of the thinkers will have been able to reconcile, to some degree, their conflicting ideas and theories."

"That would be progress," I said.

"You have my word, Mrs. Weber, that I will do everything in my power to protect your husband from those who would do him harm and prevent him from doing injury to others," Holmes added.

"I can't thank you enough," said Mrs. Weber. "You have my undying gratitude."

"Please don't tell anyone you've been to see me. My colleague Dr. Watson and I must proceed with great tact and it is imperative that nobody knows that we are involved in this matter."

"I promise that I'll not say anything to anyone," she said. "You have my word."

"Good," said Holmes. "Now you must return to your husband and minister to him as best you can. If, by chance, you see either me or Watson, at the conference or any place else, it is imperative that you do not show that you recognize us."

She got up to leave. "I'm most grateful to you, Mr. Holmes," she said. "I'll pay you whatever you wish, of course."

"You may think of my efforts, my dear lady, as my personal contribution to the subject of the forthcoming conference—social progress," Holmes said, as he held open the door.

The scientific treatment of value judgments may not only understand and empathically analyze the desired ends and the ideals which underline them; it can also "judge" them critically. This criticism can . . . be no more than a formal logical judgment of historically given value judgments and ideas, a testing of the ideals according to the postulate of the internal *consistency* of the desired end. . . . It can assist [the acting person] in becoming aware of the ultimate standards of value which he does not make explicit to himself, or which he must presuppose in order to be logical. . . . As to whether the person expressing these value judgments *should* adhere to these ultimate standards is his personal affair; it involves will and conscience, not empirical knowledge.

Max Weber.
Quoted in Edward Shils
and Henry Finch, eds.,
*Max Weber on the
Methodology of the
Social Sciences* (54).

chapter two

SHERLOCK HOLMES
Consulting Detective

When she had left,

Holmes returned to his chair with a most determined look on his face.

"I feel great sympathy for that poor woman," he told me. "She has a most terrible burden. When a person's mind is overtaken by demons, it is a frightful thing and I'm afraid that her husband may be in great danger . . . possibly from others, but more likely from himself. If you will excuse me for a short while, Watson, I must do some thinking and I'll do so while I play my violin. Please avail yourself of the newspapers I have purchased."

Then, Holmes picked up his violin and played a few memorized bars of Vivaldi melodies while I took advantage of the interlude to read the newspapers. There were numerous articles on the conference's many famous and controversial professors and thinkers, such as Vladimir Lenin and Sigmund Freud, who would be lecturing over the next five days. Holmes often played the violin when he had to work through some problem. In the middle of a particularly pleasant passage, he stopped.

"Watson," he announced, "I now know what we must do. I will arrange for us to be at that party at Claridge's."

"But Holmes, we weren't invited," I reminded him.

"Not as guests, Watson. We will help serve the guests. The owner of Claridge's has taken advantage of my services in the past and it will be no problem to arrange for us to be put on as part of the staff. We will, of course, disguise ourselves. Mrs. Weber won't give us away but others may recognize us. Please remember to bring your medical bag and your trusty revolver, though it is not likely that you will have need for either of them. The speakers at this conference fight with one another a great deal, but, up to this point, only with words. Still, we must be cognizant of Professor Weber's mental problems and the possibility that there might be some deranged or criminal person who will attempt an act of violence."

"What time will we be going to Claridge's?"

"At six o'clock, precisely," Holmes replied. "And until that time, I have much work to do."

"And what manner of work, if I may be so bold as to ask?"

Holmes smiled indulgently. "My good Watson. We are dealing here with men and women of prodigious intellectual abilities who, if the articles in the newspapers are correct, have written many important theoretical works in this new science of sociology and in related fields. When you are dealing with theorists, it is a good idea to know their theories, so as to gain some manner of understanding what motivates them and what we might expect at Mrs. Webb's party. So I will go to the Royal Library and read some books by these estimable men and women. And I shall purchase some of their books at a bookstore. I already have some of them due to my interest in the subject."

"An excellent idea, Holmes," I said.

"The theory always helps explain the theorist," Holmes instructed me, "though good Dr. Freud, who is also here for the conference and whom I have had the privilege of meeting a number of times, would, most likely, put things the other way around."

"Freud? I've always thought his ideas are quite fanciful . . . almost fairy tales," I argued. "His notion that we have a segment of our mind which he calls the *unconscious,* which we cannot know but which shapes our behavior, strikes me as terribly far-fetched. And his theories about the Oedipal Complex, that children desire their parents of the opposite sex, and the importance of childhood and sexuality . . . I most confess that I find these ideas simply scandalous. I've also read some Freud, Holmes. As a physician I thought I should. But his book on dreams strikes me as absurd. . . . It reads more like a novel than a work of science. It is fascinating, full of ideas, but I do not find it convincing. His notion that dreams are wish-fulfillments I find particularly difficult to accept. The only thing you and Freud have in common, I believe, is that the two of you share a dependency on . . ." I hesitated to say the word, for it has always pained me to see my good friend resorting to this insidious chemical.

"Cocaine," Holmes finished for me. "You don't have to mince your words, Watson. We share that, I admit, though we have different professions. But I think you may be too hard on the man. There are many who think he has made extremely important contributions with his new science of psychoanalysis. It may be too early to know whether he is a charlatan or a genius. But I believe the latter is the correct evaluation."

With that, Holmes began to clear the test tubes, microscopes, and other tools piled on his desk. After much work, he had an open space large enough to hold a book and writing pad.

"Watson," he declared, "I shall stop being an expert and become a student again, but at an age when I can enjoy and really appreciate my studies and when I can have every expectation that they will be of considerable importance. Most students, Watson, cannot say that. They are too young and too immature to appreciate the opportunities they have. So I shall become a student of social theory and see if I can learn something about the minds of the luminaries who will be at the conference and at Beatrice Webb's party. She's a champion of the working classes but comes from a wealthy family. Some might find that strange, but I do not. Life is always a great deal stranger than anything we might imagine and has its twists and turns that we can never anticipate."

"I will be going," I said. "I'll be back tomorrow at six o'clock."

"Very fine, Watson," replied Holmes.

I could not help but wonder about Holmes's remark that he knew Freud and had met with him numerous times. Could Freud, somehow, have treated Holmes? Had Holmes, who seemed so self-reliant and possessed of such a powerful will and intellect, have needed Freud's so-called talking cure? The idea struck me as outlandish . . . and yet, I could imagine that Holmes's single-mindedness and incredible intelligence may have exacted a heavy burden on what Freud would call Holmes's "psyche." That might explain why Holmes had defended Freud.

It seemed hard to believe, but, on the other hand, there were reasons to suspect that Holmes might have been, at one time or another, a patient of Freud's. Something to think about. And now Holmes was to study another new science, sociology. A most curious situation.

It is not true . . . that human activity can be released from all restraint. Nothing in the world can enjoy such a privilege. All existence being a part of the universe is relative to the remainder; its nature and method of manifestation accordingly depend not only on itself but on other beings, who consequently restrain and regulate it. Here there are only differences of degree and form between the mineral realm and the thinking person. Man's characteristic privilege is that the bond he accepts is not physical but moral; that is, social. He is governed not by a material environment brutally imposed on him, but by a conscience superior to his own, the superiority of which he feels. Because the greater part of his existence transcends the body, he escapes the body's yoke, but is subject to that of society.

But when society is disturbed by some painful crisis or by beneficent but abrupt transitions, it is momentarily incapable of exercising this influence; thence come the sudden rises in the curve of suicides.

Emile Durkheim,
Suicide: A Study in Sociology, trans. J. A. Spaulding and G. Simpson (250).

chapter **three**

Just as I was about to leave

Holmes's apartment, there was an insistent rapping on the hallway door.

"I suppose Mrs. Weber has returned for some reason," I offered. "Perhaps she has had a change of mind?"

"No, my dear Watson," replied Holmes. "That is not Mrs. Weber. When she knocked on my door, the sound was very faint . . . the knocking of a woman. This knocking is much louder and more insistent . . . it is that of a man, you may be sure . . . a man who is probably worried about something."

When Holmes opened the door, there was a man with a bushy mustache and a neatly trimmed beard standing in the hallway. He wore a finely tailored suit, though the cut was not English, and gave every indication of being a person of consequence—and one with a great awareness of his own worth.

"You must forgive me for calling upon you like this, without notifying you earlier that I would be coming," he said, in a slight French accent, "But I come with a matter of some urgency."

"Won't you come in," said Holmes. "This is my esteemed colleague, Dr. John Watson," he added, waving toward me.

The man entered the apartment. He took off his hat and at Holmes's bidding sat down.

"Thank you so much for seeing me. My name is Emile Durkheim. I am here in London to attend a conference on social progress that is to begin shortly. Perhaps you have read about it in the newspapers?"

"Indeed, I have," said Holmes. "If you will observe the large number of newspapers stacked on my table, you can see that I have been very much interested in this conference. Reporting on the conference has almost driven out the crime news. Anything that attracts a large number of very important professors and writers gets written about in considerable detail in the London press."

"Yes, yes," said Durkheim. "I'm here because of a conversation I had earlier today with one of the featured speakers—a conversation that has caused me much concern. My wife did not accompany me to this conference, because she is ill. So this afternoon, feeling the need for some exercise, I decided to take a short walk and get some air. I happened upon Max Weber in the lobby at Claridge's Hotel."

"Please continue," said Holmes, settling languidly back into his armchair.

"Since you've been reading the papers, you are aware that Max Weber is a world-famous social theorist from Germany who has made many important contributions to the science of sociology."

"I've read some of his writings," said Holmes. "I find them extremely interesting and enormously suggestive. The same applies to your works . . . some of which I've had the pleasure of reading."

"Very fine," said Durkheim, who seemed surprised by Holmes's statement. "That may help. I am worried about him . . . very worried. You probably are unaware of his psychological problems, but he has been most unstable for a goodly number of years.

He has been severely depressed and unable to lecture, though in the last few years he has improved. Or so I believed. But when I chatted with him, he seemed, for some reason, to be unusually despondent and I received the distinct impression that he may be contemplating suicide."

"Suicide?!" said Holmes, with a slight tone of surprise in his voice.

"Yes," replied Durkheim. "He told me that he felt lonely and unloved, though he has a lovely and very caring wife, and that he was upset because he was estranged from his colleagues at his university by his beliefs and his various psychological problems. Because he hasn't taught very much in recent years, he hasn't gathered around him a group of students and followers and hasn't founded what might be described as a 'school' of social theory. So he feels terribly isolated. After our talk, I went looking for his wife, Marianne, but she was not around. And so I decided that I would come to ask for your help, as you are a detective of the highest reputation and this matter needs someone with consummate tact."

"I thank you for your kind words," said Holmes.

"He needs to be protected from himself," said Durkheim. "And in his state, I fear he is capable of doing great harm to others as well."

"You think he is considering *suicide* because he is depressed?" I asked.

"Suicide," Durkheim replied, "is not well understood by the general public. Some suicide is an example of what I have called anomic behavior—the behavior of individuals or groups that do not follow the norms of society, or cannot because the norms are shifting or unclear. These individuals become detached from society, and thus are susceptible to behavior such as suicide or, conversely, indulging in criminal activities. Literally speaking, the term 'anomie' means no norms or disorder and involves a lack of solidarity and social ties. I have shown, in regard to suicide, that while individuals commit suicide, it is very much a social phenomenon."

"Suicide a social phenomenon?" I repeated in surprise. "Even if it is individuals who commit suicide?"

"Yes, Dr. Watson," he replied. "You see, my research has shown that in societies which have a great deal of integration and interaction among its members, where individual differences are minimized and there is a considerable amount of consensus on values and beliefs, in societies characterized by what I have called 'mechanical solidarity,' there are low rates of suicide. On the other hand, in societies where individual differences are maximized and there is little consensus, in societies characterized by what I have called 'organic solidarity,' there are much higher rates of suicides.

"I believe there are actually four different kinds of suicide. Some suicide is what I call 'egoistic,' which happens when the bonds that hold people together become loosened too much, when people lose any sense of obligation to others. This is, I believe, Weber's affliction. There is also 'anomic suicide,' which happens when the norms of society break down or are unclear. On the other hand, when there is excessive regulation of individuals and the demands of society are too burdensome for people, or when people have very strong group bonds and have a sense of obligation to others, you find what I call 'altruistic suicide.' This is often the case when people have strong religious convictions or certain social demands are placed upon them. And finally there is also 'fatalistic suicide' in which a sense of hopelessness drives people to suicide.

"So, while it is always individuals who commit suicide, the likelihood that any individual will do so is tied to social factors such as the person's social background. You see, I am trying to minimize the role of strictly psychological factors in understanding human behavior. I don't know whether we can ever understand the ultimate causes of people's behavior, but we can find important connections between behavior and social phenomena.

"I am interested in what I have described as 'social facts,' which can be understood as every way of acting, fixed or not, capable of exercising on an individual an external constraint. Social facts are things that exist outside of ourselves and independently of the consciousness of individuals. Society is formed, in essence, by combining the consciousness of individuals into something we might call our collective consciousness.

"This means that society is something that is both beyond us or outside of us and something that is also in ourselves at the same time. We are individuals but we are also social beings. Thus suicide is to be understood by the nature of the society in which an individual lives and the individual's social background and not, primarily, in the consciousness of an individual who commits suicide.

"If instead of seeing individual acts of suicide as separate occurrences, unrelated to one another and to be studied separately, the suicides committed in a given society during a given time period are taken as a whole, it appears that this total is not simply a sum of independent units, a collective total, but is itself a new fact sui generis, with its own unity, individuality, and consequently its own nature—a nature, furthermore, dominantly social."

"I must confess, Professor Durkheim" I said, "I find it hard to think this way. That may be because I am a physician and am used to treating individuals, each of whom has distinctive medical problems."

"It may be true, Dr. Watson," admitted Durkheim, "that individuals have their own distinctive medical problems, but think about the fact that there are occasional outbreaks of illnesses, such as the plague or smallpox, that have killed millions of people and there are other times where large numbers of people are affected by the outbreak of some disease. So some illnesses are transmitted by contagion . . . and others are caused by social factors such as malnutrition.

"In my view, society—or, more precisely, the 'collective consciousness' created in a given society—is always present in the individual and my research has suggested to me that it is religion that plays the major role in creating in individuals the beliefs that makes them adhere to society's requirements. I have suggested that we can divide the world into two realms—the sacred and the profane. The sacred is the world of religion, the profane is the everyday world—of work and family life—where religious considerations do not seem to play a role. A religion, as I define it, is a system of beliefs and practices relative to sacred things, that is to say things set apart and forbidden, beliefs and practices which unite in one single moral community called a church, all those who adhere to them. Where you have religion, you must have some kind of church.

"I have found that suicide rates tend to be low in Catholic countries, where people are held together by religious beliefs, and high in Protestant countries, where people are more or less left to their own devices and religion is a much more individualistic matter. Religion, I have come to believe, is not only a social creation but should also be seen as a transcendental or ideational representation of society. The sacred is the realm of religion, and where you have religion you always have a church. The profane, on the other hand, is the realm of society—the realm of work and play and our everyday activities. But what is important to recognize here, is that the realm of the sacred affects the realm of the profane. Most people, of course, are unaware that such is the case.

"That is because, I suggest, the fundamental categories of thought are also of religious origin. It may be said that nearly all of the great social institutions have been born in religion. If religion has given birth to all that is essential in society, it is because the *idea* of religion is the soul of religion. Religious forces are therefore human forces, moral forces."

"Then, Professor Durkheim, is there no place for freedom?" I asked. "That would seem to be the logical import of your theories. If religion plays the dominant role in giving man his moral sensibilities and desire to adhere to society's strictures, how do you account for freedom?"

"No, Dr. Watson," Durkheim replied. "That is not the case. Men are free but they are not absolutely free—nor can they be. People must respect the rules of society. Otherwise you have anarchy, in which case people end up being less free than when obeying society's rules."

He began to lecture, as if to his students. "Man's characteristic privilege is that the bond he accepts is not physical but moral; this is, social. He is governed not by a material environment brutally imposed on him, but by a conscience superior to his own, the superiority of which he feels. Because the greater part of his existence transcends the body, he escapes the body's yoke, but is subject to that of society.

"Those who do not accept society's norms, as I have explained earlier, I term anomic or normless. Not all anomic people commit suicide, however. Some become criminals. We simply cannot be free of every restraint. What is unique about men are the checks to which they are subjected are not physical but moral, that is social. When, as a result of calamities or great social dislocations, the restraints that ordinarily hold people in check are not adequate, we find anomie and with it, phenomena such as suicide and *deviance*.

"Crime, then, has an interesting hidden function. It brings together upright consciences and concentrates them. By this I mean that crime offers a scapegoat for society's ills. Having deviants to point one's finger at is functional in that it enables the general social group to find a sense of unity and to solidify its moral and its social identity. Great crimes lead to a heightened sense of moral outrage and to a greater sense of solidarity and identification with one's society. I'm very much interested in criminal behavior and the effect is has upon people who are at the scene of the crime. That is something I am doing research on now.

"Thus, I have argued that deviance has a certain function as far as the maintenance of group morals and group solidarity are concerned, for deviants remind us of how we are different from them. This suggests that the real reason we put criminals in jail is not to rehabilitate them but as a means of reaffirming our moral superiority and that of our society."

"I find that notion very interesting," admitted Holmes. "But in the course of my long career, I have often come in contact with criminals who didn't seem to seek success but had other motivations, it would seem. Some killers were motivated by jealousy or insane hatred, and not hope of financial gain."

"That is quite likely, Mr. Holmes," the professor agreed. "Remember, I am dealing with society in general and groups of people, not individuals. We sociologists focus our attention on society, in general, and what people do as members of groups and organizations. What you are talking about is, in large measure, dealt with by psychologists. The division of labor, which I believe has been involved in the change from mechanical to organic solidarity, plays an important role here. When society was characterized by mechanical solidarity, there was little anomie. Now that society is characterized by organic solidarity, as represented by the growth of large and impersonal corporations, the bands which used to hold people together have been broken. There is much more anomie. What I have called the collective consciousness, which unifies people in terms of their beliefs and morals, has been weakened immeasurably, if not broken into a thousand pieces."

"So, Professor Durkheim," Holmes replied, leaning back in his chair, "criminals, according to your theory, are, in a sense, ultimately useful to society. And I, who have devoted my life to foiling criminals, am actually, your theory would suggest, harming society. I am, of course, pushing your argument to absurd lengths, but I cannot help but saying I find it most entertaining. I am, from your point of view, as you would put it, a dysfunctional person. Quite amusing!" He could not restrain himself and burst out laughing.

Durkheim smiled faintly, more polite than amused.

"Not quite, for in capturing criminals, you enable societies to find people—wrongdoers of one sort or another—to whom everyone can feel morally superior, and thus you actually help promote social solidarity. If I have been able to edify you as well as entertain and amuse you, all the better," pronounced Durkheim. "That, I have often thought, is what professors should do."

"To get back to the subject of your visit," said Holmes, standing up. "I will do what I can to prevent Professor Weber from causing harm to himself or to others. You have my word, Professor Durkheim."

"I cannot thank you enough," he said. "I shall be pleased to pay you whatever you may want for this service."

"Thank you, for your kind offer, professor," said Holmes. "But I will not require remuneration for my efforts or those of my companion, Watson."

"I have one other favor to ask. I have here," Durkheim said, taking an envelope from his pocket, "a sealed envelope in which you will find a letter I have written to you. I ask you not to open the envelope and read the letter until I request you to do so.

I think you will find it of considerable interest. Can I count on you to do this?"

"Of course," replied Holmes, taking the envelope and turning it over and over in his hands. "Neither I nor Watson will read the contents of this letter until you have asked us to do so. I give you my word."

"Good," said Professor Durkheim.

With that exchange, he left.

"Durkheim sees crime as caused by social factors," I told Holmes, "but I cannot help but wonder whether there are physical factors involved as well."

"Such as?" asked Holmes.

"I have often thought that the brain's prefrontal cortex may be implicated in criminal behavior. It controls what might be described as our higher intellectual functions . . . by which I mean reasoning, judgment, and impulse control. Certain parts of the prefrontal cortex are involved with anger and there may well be problems with the prefrontal cortex's ability to provide restraint-producing or inhibitory factors in our minds, which are behind the impulsive behavior of criminals."

"That is a most interesting hypothesis, Watson," said Holmes, "and one that strikes me as helping us understand criminal behavior. One thing that sociologists do not consider adequately, so it seems, is the human mind, about which the good doctor Freud has much to say. They also neglect, as well, the biological components of behavior. Sociologists, seeing man as a social animal, tend to see crime as essentially a social phenomenon. Durkheim has explained that crime is connected to deviance and Weber might possibly see criminal behavior as a perversion of ascetic Protestantism's focus on material wealth. Du Bois would connect it to the issue of race and Webb, no doubt, to poverty.

"But why some individuals become criminals and others do not is, indeed, a mystery. The criminals we have apprehended, Watson, have come from every class and every profession. I leave it for the sociologists and others to determine why people become criminals. Our task is to catch criminals and to put them behind prison bars. That is one important step toward social progress."

In the field of its highest development, in the United States, the pursuit of wealth, stripped of its religious and ethical meaning, tends to become associated with purely mundane passions, which often actually give it the character of sport.

No one knows who will live in this cage in the future or whether at the end of this tremendous development entirely new prophets will arise, or there will be a great birth of old ideas and ideals, or, if neither, mechanized petrification, embellished with a sort of convulsive self-importance. For of the last stage of this cultural development, it might well be truly said, "Specialists without spirit, sensualists without heart; this nullity imagines that it has attained a level of civilization never before achieved."

Max Weber, *The Protestant Ethic and the Spirit of Capitalism* (182).

chapter **four**

I had just begun what I believed would be

a leisurely breakfast with my wife, the next morning, when the maid appeared with a telegraph from Holmes. I set down my fork and tore open the envelope.

"Come immediately," Holmes wrote. "There is an emergency involving the social theorists."

"Good lord," I thought. "Something terrible must have happened last night."

I nearly scalded myself with my cup of tea and rushed through my toast with strawberry preserves. Calling a goodbye to my wife, I hurried off to the apartment where Holmes lived. When I reached 221B Baker Street, I found Inspector Lestrade of Scotland Yard there, pacing back and forth. Holmes was sitting down, his eyes closed and his left hand on his forehead, deep in thought. On a table, I could see a number of sociology books from Holmes's bookshelves, which lay open and underlined, with copious notes in the margins. Some were still lying beside the bookseller's paper wrapping, as if Holmes had just bought them the previous evening. There was a volume, *The Protestant Ethic and the Spirit of Capitalism,* by Max Weber and another work, *The Division of Labor in Society,* by Emile Durkheim. Georg Simmel's *Sociology* was also

there, along with another of his books, *The Philosophy of Money.*
W. E. B. Du Bois's *The Soul of Black Folk* shared space with a pam-
phlet by Lenin, *What is to be done?* There was another of Lenin's
books, *Materialism and Empirio-Criticism,* and several other books
as well, too many for me to catch the titles. Many of them had
slips of paper in them, in various places, and sheets of paper
written with lengthy notes lay beside them.

"Lestrade," I exclaimed, shaking his hand. "What brings
you here? Has something happened to one of the sociologists who
came to London for the conference?" I did not wish to give away
my knowledge of Professor Weber's problems.

"Yes," explained Lestrade. "Something astonishing has happened. It seems that last night a group of these sociologists, the
main speakers at the conference, got together for dinner in a private
suite at Claridge's restaurant. There was Max Weber and his wife,
Marianne, from Germany. I believe it was Weber's wife who had
suggested that the speakers all should have dinner together. And
there was another German sociologist there as well . . . Georg Simmel. His wife didn't attend as she was visiting a friend. I take it that
Weber and Simmel were good friends. They were joined by a
French sociologist, Emile Durkheim, who was in England by himself. His wife, I take it, was ill, so he came to London alone. A famous Negro sociologist named Du Bois and a Russian revolutionary
named Lenin were also there. They also were alone, as was
Sigmund Freud. I believe Lenin is a Communist. And they had
invited Beatrice Webb, the famous feminist thinker. Her husband,
Sidney, couldn't make it, I understand, so she brought a friend,
Lady Cecily Bracknell, who directs the Bracknell Foundation. It
seems, curiously, that many of the people at the dinner party had
applied to her foundation for money. For worthy causes, of course."

"The conversation must have been remarkable," I said.
"Some of the finest minds of our time dining together."

"There's more to tell," said Lestrade. "It was just after everyone had finished dinner. They were standing around, getting ready to leave, when it seems that Weber and Durkheim and some of the other social theorists there got into a discussion about sociology and politics . . . or whatever . . . and, as I understand it, Durkheim attacked Weber's theories in a rather intemperate manner. Weber, who is a large, powerful man, and, it seems, somewhat unstable, psychologically speaking, lost his self-control and ended up punching Durkheim in the face. On the left cheek. Everyone then tried to restrain Weber, who seemed to be raving mad at the moment. Then, Lady Bracknell fainted from the shock of it all. She was caught by a waiter, just before she fell to the ground. The men instantly crowded around to help her. It was very chaotic. She slowly came back to consciousness and Weber, Lenin, and Simmel helped her to a chair while Durkheim ran into the kitchen and brought her a towel with ice in it to help revive her."

"How terrible," I replied.

"There's worse to come," said Lestrade gloomily. "Freud, who is a physician, rushed over to examine her. He felt her pulse and asked her a few questions. She seemed to be all right. A short time later, Lady Bracknell uttered a loud scream. 'My diamond,' she shouted, 'Something's happened to my diamond!' She had been wearing a large diamond jewel attached to a thin, gold chain around her neck. Everyone started looking for it on the floor; they did find the chain but they couldn't find the diamond. The Bracknell diamond is a very beautiful brilliant stone and is worth a small fortune. Lady Bracknell loves it and hardly goes anywhere without it. It has sentimental value, she says . . . since it was given to her by her late husband, Ernest. It is insured for a great deal of money, but Lady Bracknell is more interested in getting her diamond back. So we have this collection of famous sociologists and social thinkers and it looks like one of them may have succumbed to temptation and stolen Lady Bracknell's diamond."

"Good lord," I cried out. "What a terrible thing!"

"The curious thing is that the hotel's detective was nearby. He got in touch with us and we sent some men over immediately. We searched everyone who had been in the room, but nobody had the diamond. It was, as you might imagine, a most delicate matter. We have some men guarding the room and the whole kitchen area. It would be a terrible scandal if it broke in the press, which is why I'm here. I've asked Holmes to do what he can to find the diamond . . . and see if we can avoid creating a scandal. The diamond has disappeared, right before our eyes, and though we've searched the premises many times, we can't find it.

"There's still worse to come," Lestrade continued. "Durkheim left the restaurant in bad shape. The left side of his face was swollen and he was holding a large piece of ice on his cheek to reduce the swelling. This morning we found Durkheim's wallet in a gutter by the Thames. He was already in a dizzy state and we fear he has been robbed and either fell or was pushed into the Thames. Our men are looking in the river now.

"If Durkheim were still alive he'd most certainly have returned to his hotel room, unless he had been injured. I imagine that he was seriously injured by Weber's blow and suffered the full effects later. We checked all the hospitals but nobody looking like Durkheim was admitted last night. I talked with Weber's wife, who informed me that she had retained Holmes. So I've come here to ask him to investigate the jewelry robbery and this matter as well. To see what he knows and whether he has any information that might be of assistance. The people at the dinner party don't know that Durkheim is dead. Even Max Weber doesn't realize what happened. Right now, though, it looks like he might be—though he doesn't realize it—Durkheim's killer. But I want to make certain that Durkheim *is* dead before I press charges. Everyone who was at the party is in a state of agitation and terribly upset about the jewel robbery and about Weber's behavior. I take it he is a very disturbed man. He may have become deranged and criminal. Things like that have been known to happen. I'm beginning to wonder whether all these sociologists are a bit crazy. Maybe they should be in a different kind of institution?

"I've asked everyone who was at the party to remain at Claridge's Hotel while I pursue my investigation of the jewel robbery. Lady Bracknell is terribly upset, but she has agreed not to say anything for the moment. We have sworn everyone else involved in the dinner to secrecy also. The people who were at the dinner party believe I am just investigating the robbery last night. I hope they are correct."

Holmes was now deep in thought. He sat quietly while Lestrade told me of the events of the previous evening.

"Lestrade," he said, lifting his head from his hands. "I will begin my investigation of the jewel robbery immediately. I want to search the hotel and interrogate all the parties involved, to get more information . . . so I can get to the bottom of this matter."

"Of course," said Lestrade. "You know how I value your abilities. Your acceptance of this case is most fortunate. It turns out that I am deeply involved with another case that I've tentatively called 'The Noble Bachelor,' so your taking this one will be a big help to me."

"You need not worry about Weber doing anything else," added Holmes. "He is probably suffering terrible remorse from his actions. His wife must have been horrified by his behavior. But time is of the essence. We want to prevent a scandal from erupting over the diamond robbery."

"And now Watson and I will go to Claridge's and interrogate everyone who was at the party. This case may not be as simple as it seems. There may be others, who we don't know about, involved in the theft of this jewel. It is possible that a team of professional thieves were at work here. The question I hope to answer is—assuming none of them were able to secrete it on their persons—where could that diamond be hidden? Then I will be able to determine who took it."

Lestrade looked relieved. "We searched the place thoroughly and searched everyone who was near the dining room—the cooks, the waiters . . . everyone. But if anyone can find Lady Bracknell's diamond, I'm sure it will be you, Holmes."

I had every confidence that Holmes could find the diamond and send the thief, or thieves, to jail before the news of the robbery leaked out and became a front-page story in the newspapers. It is possible but most unlikely, I thought, that one of the famous sociologists actually stole the jewel. If so, there would be a terrific scandal. But there was no detective in England who was Holmes's equal and he had a genius for solving crimes that seemed, to everyone else, insoluble.

"Good luck with your interviews," Lestrade said as he left.

"Thank you, Lestrade," said Holmes. "Professors are never easy to deal with. They are either difficult to pry information out of, because they are terribly afraid they will say something wrong and get caught doing so, or they are just the opposite . . . and talk endlessly, mostly about themselves, their ideas, and their accomplishments. They are full of improbable theories and often become involved in absurd experiments. Most of them, I have found, are simply insufferable."

"Holmes," I said. "You've only been a student one day and you've already picked up many of the antipathies students have toward professors."

"Yes, you're right, my good Watson. I'm afraid nobody likes professors except themselves . . . and possibly their wives and children. And now, let us be off to Claridge's Hotel and see what we can learn from the little gathering of world-famous luminaries who were at the party last night."

Holmes had a slight smile on his face and did not seem terribly perturbed by the events Lestrade had described. I wondered whether that was because of his tremendous sense of confidence . . . or whether he already knew something I did not know.

The desire for money is the permanent disposition that the mind displays in an established money economy. Accordingly, the psychologist simply cannot ignore the frequent lament that money is the God of our times. Or course, he can only linger on it and discover significant relationships between the two ideas because it is the privilege of psychology not to commit blasphemy. The concept of God has its deeper essence in the fact that all the varieties and contrasts of the world reach unity in it, that is the *coincidentia oppositorium*, in the beautiful phrase of Nicholas of Cusa, that peculiarly modern spirit of the waning Middle Ages. It is this idea that all the strange and irreconciled aspects of being find unity and harmony, from which stem the peace, the security and the all-encompassing richness of feeling, which are part of the idea of God and the idea that we possess Him.

The feelings stimulated by money have a psychological similarity to this in their own arena. By increasingly becoming the absolutely sufficient expression and equivalent of all values, it rises in a very abstract elevation over the whole broad variety of objects; it becomes the centre in which the most opposing, alien and distant things find what they have in common and touch each other.

Georg Simmel, "Money
in Modern Culture."

chapter five

WE ARRANGED TO MEET
WITH LADY BRACKNELL FIRST.

Holmes and I arrived at Claridge's Hotel

early in the morning and arranged with the manager to have a room where we could question each of the people involved in the tumultuous party. In the meantime, we went over the dining room, replaying the steps of the evening. A faint stain on the mantelpiece was more than familiar from my medical training, not to mention my time as a military surgeon in the Afghan campaign.

"Blood," I called over to Holmes.

He examined the spot. "You see the oblong shape of the splash, do you not, Watson? Durkheim must have stood about a foot in this direction, while Weber hit him from this angle. Thank you for your acute perception—that helps me quite a bit."

After finishing with the blood spot, Holmes returned to his earlier project. He was dropping a child's marble onto the rug where Lady Bracknell had fainted and letting it roll around the room. The marble was not quite as large as the diamond, but Holmes seemed to be satisfied that it would mimic the diamond's path around the room. He spent several minutes chasing the marble into corners on his hands and knees. If I didn't know Holmes so well, I would have been embarrassed to see a grown man in that position.

We also made a quick tour through the kitchen and pantries. In the ice room, Holmes pointed to a block of ice with one corner chipped away.

"Inexpertly chipped," Holmes said. "Perhaps one of the waiters is new, or perhaps someone else has been in here." He pulled his watch from his pocket. "We may need to examine this ice further. However, we should now get back to questioning the distinguished thinkers."

We arranged to meet with Lady Bracknell first. A police-man knocked on the door and let her in. The poor woman looked terrible. Her eyes were all red, as if she had been crying all night. She entered slowly and sat in the seat Holmes offered. She was a slender woman of about seventy, with fine features, who was dressed in a handsome, beautifully tailored, gray dress.

"You cannot realize how pleased I am that you are on this case, Mr. Holmes," she said. "If anyone can solve this terrible crime, I'm sure it is you. With the aid, of course, of your compan-ion Dr. Watson." She nodded at me.

"Have no fear, Lady Bracknell . . . I shall get to the bottom of this and restore your diamond to you. If the diamond is on the premises, hidden somewhere, I shall find it. And if it isn't here, I'll find it—wherever it might be!"

"Oh, thank you, Mr. Holmes," the good woman said. "That diamond is my pride and joy. It was given to me by my late hus-band, Ernest, and I wear it all the time to remind me of him, though some people have cautioned me against doing so, since it is so valuable. We were married for forty-five years before he passed away. It is insured for twenty thousand pounds, but I would much prefer to have my diamond back . . . as you can well understand."

"Yes, I see," said Holmes. "But tell me how it was that you were asked to attend the dinner last night."

"I'm a very good friend of Beatrice Webb. I fund some of her projects with money from the foundation I run. It turns out that a number of the scholars at the party had also submitted requests for funds. All except Dr. Freud and Mr. Lenin, if I remember correctly. So I wanted to have the opportunity to meet them and gain some sense of their stature and determine whether it would be prudent to fund their projects.

"It so happened that we were all seated around a round table, with a beautiful ice sculpture of a swan in the middle of it. Professor Weber was seated to my left and Professor Durkheim to my right. Professor Simmel was seated next to Professor Weber and then next to him was my dear friend Beatrice. Next came Mr. Lenin, Dr. Freud, and Dr. Du Bois. The dinner gave me an opportunity to chat with everyone. The food, of course, was superb and so was the service."

"Several of them had submitted requests for funds. That strikes me as quite remarkable," I said.

"Not really, Dr. Watson. My foundation receives numerous requests for all kinds of people for worthy projects. The professors all had very fine studies in mind. The problem, of course, is that my foundation has limited resources and I can't fund every worthy project."

"Could you tell me," asked Holmes, who seemed very interested in the information she was providing, "what each of the professors wanted to do with any money your foundation might provide. This information may have some bearing on the matter at hand."

"Of course," replied Lady Bracknell. "I'm getting old and somewhat feeble, but my mind is as sharp as it ever was. The French professor, Mr. Durkheim, wanted to start a new scholarly press to publish books investigating suicide, criminal behavior, and other social problems. The subject is a very important one but funding scholarly presses is a bit far removed from our interests, I'm afraid. Professor Simmel wanted to start an institute to investigate what he described as 'everyday life.' He explained that most sociologists have lofty theories about institutions and groups, but nobody had spent much time analyzing the ordinary things people do in their everyday lives—what they eat, who they talk to, what they do on their jobs, how they amuse themselves—that kind of thing. His application was quite interesting, I must say, but I don't see how it will lead to the amelioration of social problems, which is the primary concern of my foundation. Dr. Du Bois sought funds to establish an institution to give scholarships so disadvantaged members of his race might attend universities, a worthy matter that we are already funding. Professor Weber wanted funding to conduct research and write a book on the relationship between religions and economic systems. It is a bit far removed from our interests, though of course it might have long-term importance. The problem I face in running my foundation is that there are too many social problems for us to fix and too many worthy applications for us to fund. But I do the best I can."

"So," said Holmes, with a look of some satisfaction on his face. "We have a number of professors who want funds, for one reason or another. The question that immediately presents itself is whether one of them, or some other person in the restaurant, seized the opportunity to obtain the funds they desired by grabbing your diamond, in a moment of weakness, no doubt, and hiding it somewhere."

"I can't believe that any of the people at the dinner could do that, Mr. Holmes," replied Lady Bracknell. "They are all people of consequence, people of great reputation. I find it hard to imagine that they would do something like that."

"You'd be surprised what people will do if they think they won't get caught, Lady Bracknell," I interjected. "Sometimes people have a momentary lapse of good sense when presented with a situation that promises to be of great financial advantage. Some philosophers have suggested that most people are moral because they've never been tempted, because they've never had the opportunity to be immoral. I've always felt that this argument has some sense to it, though our sociologist friends would probably argue that immoral people haven't been properly socialized or are living in a period of turmoil when everyone's sense of right and wrong has been disrupted."

"I hope you are wrong, Dr. Watson," she replied. "But, of course, you and Mr. Holmes have had a great deal of experience with criminals. And I have not, fortunately . . . or at least not until last night, that is."

"You are a brave and good woman," said Holmes. "I am impressed with the work you do with your foundation. The professors and scholars you met are here to talk about social progress, but I can see that you are actually doing something to facilitate it. Rest assured, you will soon have your diamond back . . . and with it, a happier and more sanguine view of the morality of men and women. You've been of considerable help to us and for that I am most grateful."

"Thank you, Mr. Holmes. I have every confidence that you will both find my diamond and justify my faith in mankind."

With that, Lady Bracknell got up and left.

"A remarkable woman," reflected Holmes, after she had gone. "Perhaps somewhat foolhardy in wearing that diamond all the time, but I take it she is not only extremely intelligent and sagacious, but also somewhat sentimental. It is our emotions that get us into trouble most of the time, Watson. How social thinkers will figure out how to deal with our emotions should be most interesting."

Modern officialdom functions in the following specific manner:

I. There is the principle of fixed and official jurisdictional areas, which are generally ordered by rules, that is, by laws or administrative regulations.

1. The regular activities required for the purposes of the bureaucratically governed structure are distributed in a fixed way as official duties.

2. The authority to give the commands required for the discharge of these duties is distributed in a stable way and is strictly delimited by rules concerning the coercive means, physical, sacerdotal, or otherwise, which may be placed at the disposal of officials.

3. Methodical provision is made for the regular and continuous fulfillment of these duties and for the execution of corresponding rights; only persons who have the generally regulated qualifications to serve are employed.

In public and lawful government these three elements constitute "bureaucratic authority." In private economic domination, they constitute bureaucratic "management." Bureaucracy, thus understood, is fully developed in political and ecclesiastical communities only in the modern state, and in the private economy, only in the most advanced institutions of capitalism.

Max Weber, *Wirtschaft und Gesselschaft*. Quoted in H. H. Gerth and C. Wright Mills, eds. and trans., *From Max Weber: Essays in Sociology*.

chapter six

MAX WEBER EXPLAINS WHY
HE PUNCHED EMILE DURKHEIM

Max Weber knocked on the door

of the room we were using and slowly opened it. He walked very slowly and was slightly stooped over. He was a large, powerful-looking man with a bushy mustache and a thick beard. I would estimate that he was around fifty years of age. His complexion was pale. He sat down on a chair slowly. He seemed, for some reason, completely devoid of energy. I had the notion to rush him to St. George's Hospital, not far from the hotel, and give him a thorough examination. But if Weber's wife was correct, his problems were psychological rather than physical.

Holmes took the initiative.

"My name is Sherlock Holmes," he explained. "I am a consulting detective and this is my associate, Dr. Watson," Holmes said, pointing to me. "I'm investigating the events that took place last night at the dinner party your wife arranged, Professor Weber," said Holmes.

"That horrible party," he said, weakly. "Not only was there a jewel robbery, that I find most mystifying, but I was terribly insulted by Emile Durkheim, who I always had thought was my friend, even though we disagree on certain things relative to the nature of sociological theory. I stress the importance of the individual actor while he focuses on social forces. We began a discussion of our theories which rapidly became very heated and this led to some angry words by Durkheim.

"For no reason that I can think of he became incensed at me. At one moment last night I had the distinct impression that he was going to try and hit me, so I punched him in the face. It was purely defensive . . . an involuntary reaction. I had been a member of a dueling society in my university days in Heidelberg and I'm afraid took action before I knew what I was doing. Fortunately, it was just a light punch. I'm afraid that the events last night—the jewelry robbery and my behavior—don't suggest that the possibilities of social progress are very promising."

He managed a weak smile in response to his own joke.

"Do you have any notion about who might have taken Lady Bracknell's diamond?" I asked. "As I understand it, when she fainted, a number of you, who were near her, raced to help her. Could one of you, perhaps in a moment of weakness, taken it?"

"Preposterous," said Weber. "Absolutely preposterous! You had in that room some of the best thinkers of the age—people of international reputation and great stature. I didn't take it and I simply can't believe that any of us could have taken it. Besides, if someone in our party did take it, where did they hide it? The police have searched the premises diligently."

"Then who do you think took it?" asked Holmes.

"It had to be one of the staff—though how they got their hands on it and what they did with it . . . where they hid it, is beyond me," replied Weber. "It probably was the waiter or someone else in the staff."

"Yes, that's a distinct possibility," agreed Holmes. "Lady Bracknell informed us that you requested a grant from her. It struck me that you might, perhaps, be short of funds and wanted some money to carry you over for a while. Is that so?"

"Not at all," replied Weber. "I have started teaching again, in a limited way, and though my finances are somewhat restricted, I am not in need of money. It would, I admit, be most helpful to have a foundation grant to augment what my university provides in the way of research funds. We professors are always looking for funds from foundations to help us with our research."

"I see," said Holmes. "I'm learning a great deal about professors lately . . . and their many needs. Let's return to the matter of your dispute with Professor Durkheim. What exactly did you argue about?"

"Professors are always arguing with one another," he replied. "You must understand that. We spend our lives trying to prove that our theories are correct and the theories of those who disagree with us are wrong. Durkheim and I got into a discussion about our views on what is most important in sociological thought. Interpretative sociology, as I see it, considers the individual and his action as the basic unit, as its basic element . . . its atom, if you will. Durkheim disagrees with this notion.

"The individual, I argue, is the sole carrier of meaningful conduct. Such concepts as the state, associations, feudalism, all designate certain categories of human interaction. But it is the task of sociology to reduce these abstract concepts to understandable action—that is, without exception, to the actions of participating individual men. Society, then, as I define it, is a collection of individuals and it is to be understood by investigating the interactions individuals have with one another."

"What distinction do you make, then, between society and sociology?" I asked. "It seems to me that with your focus on individuals, society is just an abstraction."

"A good question," Weber replied. He was becoming more animated. "I've just said something about what society is . . . it is, I suggest, a name for a collection of individuals. Sociology, as I see it, and my definition is somewhat technical in nature, is a science which attempts the interpretive understanding of social action in order to arrive at an explanation of its causes, its course, and its effects. This action may be either overt or purely inward or subjective. It may consist of positive intervention in a situation or of deliberately refraining from such intervention or passively acquiescing in the situation. That is, in certain situations where one is expected to act, not doing anything is a kind of action.

"Action is social insofar as, by virtue of the subjective meaning attached to it by the acting individual or individuals, it takes account of the behavior of others and is thereby oriented in its course. It's the meaning actions have for people that are important and the shared values and interests individuals have with one another that are crucial. For example, what we call the state is really not an autonomous entity but rather a way, involving certain areas of our lives, that individuals act and react with one another. A state is a human community that successfully claims the monopoly of legitimate physical force within a given territory.

"Can you follow me?" he asked.

"I believe so," I replied. To tell the truth, I wasn't terribly clear about what the professor believed. I have trouble following theoretical arguments.

"So, your striking Professor Durkheim is to be understood as a sociologically significant action, I take it," said Holmes.

Weber blanched. He waited for a minute to collect his thoughts.

"I deeply regret my behavior," he said. "But let us return to the matter of what precipitated that action. Durkheim's notion of what sociology involves is the opposite of mine. He has what I consider to be simplistic ideas about some vague collective consciousness that exists both outside of individual consciousness and above it, that is permanent and crystallizes into ideas that in some mysterious way are communicated to everyone. They furnish the mind, he believes, with molds that shape thought and behavior. I would have none of it. He believes, in effect, that society shapes individual behavior. He writes about collective representations, by which he means the ideas that people hold in common, and some kind of a collective consciousness, a combination of the consciousness of individuals that lead to a society. He wants to start a book publishing house to popularize his ideas. He seems rather desperate to do so.

"In addition," Weber continued, "Durkheim believes in what we sociologists call 'functionalism.' He argues that when we seek to explain a social phenomenon, we must examine the cause or action which produces it and the function it fulfills. He uses the term 'function' instead of 'end' or 'purpose' because social phenomena, for him, are to be examined in terms of their functions and the role they play in maintaining society, or, conversely, in the case of dysfunctional behavior, leading to social disorganization. He believes we have to determine whether there is a functional relation between the fact under consideration and the general needs of society.

"To my mind, this is sheer rubbish and totally inadequate to understand human social behavior. The organic school, to which Durkheim belongs, attempts to understand social interaction by using, as a point of departure, the 'whole' within which the individual acts. His actions and behavior are then interpreted somewhat in the way that a physiologist would treat the role of an organ of the body in the 'economy' of that organism, that is from the point of view of the survival of the latter.

"This functional frame of reference is convenient for purposes of practical illustration . . . but it is only the beginning of sociological analysis as I see things . . . not the end of it. To offer a correct causal interpretation of an action, you have to examine both the action itself and the motives of the individuals involved in the action. Durkheim's ideas, you must realize, have been rejected, for the most part by sociologists," added Weber. "His ideas are passé. For all practical purposes, metaphorically speaking, we can say, with some confidence, that Durkheim is dead!"

"Durkheim is dead?" asked Holmes, with a tone of astonishment in his voice. He was clearly surprised by that statement. "Isn't that a bit harsh?"

"His ideas are popular in France, perhaps . . . but in the wider world, few scholars take them seriously. Durkheim is too deterministic. He leaves little room for human intelligence or the moral sensibility," said Weber.

"Have you, by chance, seen Durkheim today? Nobody's seen him since your altercation last night, when he staggered out of the hotel," said Holmes. "Do you have any idea about where he might be?"

"No, I haven't seen him," said Weber. "I am not his chaperone . . . and have not made it my business to look for him. I feel ashamed about having struck him. I'm sure you can understand that. So, though I have not avoided him, I also have not sought him out. He may be keeping away from people, also . . . because he's upset about last night . . . or not feeling well."

I must confess that I thought Weber's statement about Durkheim being "dead" shocking, for reasons that are quite obvious. I found it very difficult to understand what Professor Weber was talking about and I was convinced that this new science of sociology, if he were one of its great theorists, would never amount to very much. But Holmes, who had been reading Weber and Durkheim and many other sociologists the previous evening, seemed to understand what he was saying and was following his arguments with great interest.

"I should inform you," Holmes said, "that as a detective, I, too, am vitally interested in motives and their relation to people's actions. For example, let's take the matter of murder."

As he said that word, Holmes was scrutinizing Weber's face, but Weber had no reaction that I could observe. Holmes, on the other hand, may have noticed some interesting reaction. Or, perhaps, to use Weber's ideas, no reaction was a kind of re-action?

"In murder cases there are often many suspects who have motives that we can discern," said Holmes, "motives that could lead them to murder, but often it is those with hidden motives who are the guilty party. Finding the hidden motive is the prob-lem. The same applies, of course, to other kinds of crime—such as jewelry robberies."

"Yes," said Weber, "I can understand that. Although human action is the core of sociological thought, there are other consider-ations as well. I dealt with the matter a few years ago in my book *The Protestant Ethic and the Spirit of Capitalism.* Perhaps you are fa-miliar with it?"

"Indeed I am," said Holmes. "I was reading it, with great interest, just last night."

At that, Weber seemed to relax a bit. He even managed an-other faint smile.

"How remarkable," he said. "In my book, as you know, I argue that there was a strong relationship between the fundamen-tal religious ideas of ascetic Protestantism and capitalism. I call this 'inner-worldly asceticism' and argue that it involved the transformation of a religious concept that was originally concerned with the religious world to the everyday world. Calvin thought that if the clergy were wealthy, it enhanced their prestige. Leisure and enjoyment were to be avoided, time was not to be wasted. And what was favored was hard, continuous bodily and mental labor, frugal living, and plain dress. Wealth was a sign that God had predestined a person for success and he was among the elect.

"There was a powerful tendency, due to Calvin's ideas, toward a kind of uniformity of life, which immensely aids the capitalistic interest in the standardization of production. This had its ideal foundations in the repudiation of all idolatry of the flesh. Puritanism had the psychological effect of freeing the acquisition of goods from the traditionalistic ethics of medieval life. It accomplished this by breaking the bounds of the impulse of acquisition by legalizing it and by looking on it as, in a sense, directly willed by God. Wealth, then, became a sign of God's blessing. And even more important, the valuation of restless, continuous, systematic work in a worldly calling became the highest means to asceticism and, as the same time, the surest and most evident proof of rebirth and genuine faith . . . leading to what can be called the spirit of capitalism. One important thing to remember is that we did not find this 'inner-worldly asceticism' in the ancient world or in non-Western religions."

"Professor Weber," I interjected. "May I ask a question here?"

"Of course," he said.

"Are you suggesting," I asked, "that Puritanism is, in some way, the source of our capitalistic economic system, and that people, though they may not be aware of doing so, are motivated to work hard and amass riches because of their religious beliefs?"

"Precisely," he said. "My theory suggests that Protestantism freed people from medieval notions about the sanctity of poverty and argued that pursuing wealth was a glorious thing, and that amassing it was a sign of God's blessing. Remember, Dr. Watson, individuals act on the basis of their beliefs. When I visited the United States, I found that the religious and ethical basis of capitalism, which stemmed from ascetic Protestantism, had been stripped away and the pursuit of wealth had now taken on the character of a sport. Originally, it was felt that this desire for external goods would lie on the shoulders of those who pursued material goods like a light cloak, but the cloak became an iron cage, and material goods have gained an increasing and finally an inexorable power over the lives of men . . . and one might venture that capitalism has escaped from its cage of religious asceticism and needs it no longer. No one knows who will live in this cage in the future.

"We must recognize, of course, that Protestant asceticism was in turn influenced by its development by the social and economic conditions in which it was found. People, of course, are unable to give religious ideas the significance for culture and national character which they deserve. What I believe is that ideas are not simply direct reflections of material interests . . . there is something I call an 'elective affinity,' by which I mean that certain social groups and ideas somehow seek one another out. I don't believe in the economic determinism of the Marxists and of people like Lenin, whose ideas are overly simplistic. It is beliefs and values that shape societies, not economic relations. The economic relations we find in a society are the result of the dominant values found in a society, not the other way around."

"But aren't you actually accepting Durkheim's notion about some kind of collective consciousness and social factors influencing individual behavior?" I challenged him. "It looks like that to me when you argue that ascetic Protestantism was instrumental in the development of capitalism."

"Not at all," he replied. "You should realize that I was using Calvin's ideas and ascetic Protestantism as what I call an 'ideal type.' Ideal types are analytical constructions I use to make sense of social behavior and various kinds of collectivities. Ideal types are made by considering many different points of view and by synthesizing a number of individual phenomena into a unified analytical construct. For example, my theory that ascetic Protestantism, at a certain period of time, led to the development of capitalism is one kind of ideal type—the kind rooted in particular historical situations. There is another kind of ideal type that is not historical but which is much more general. For example, I have written a good deal on the notion of *bureaucracies.*"

"Bureaucrats . . . how I despise them," I said with a shudder. "At the hospital where I see patients, there are endless rules and regulations that our directors and their minions keep generating. These administrators are making life impossible for me to practice medicine intelligently."

"But it would be worse without any rules," replied Weber. "Bureaucracies have certain characteristics. They are found in all organizations, they separate the private life of a person from his role in the bureaucracy, they formulate rules that are meant to cover all possibilities, and are, in essence, rational and objective, and based on expertise of individuals in whatever level of the bureaucracy they have achieved. As bad as bureaucracies might seem, life would be a great deal worse without them. They help stabilize societies and provide people with the sense that they will all be treated the same; that is, fairly, and that personal influence will not be of any importance."

"I find that difficult to accept," disagreed Holmes. "In principle, bureaucracies may work the way you have explained them, but in practice, I have always found that people find ways to get around the rules and regulations."

"That is true," Weber admitted. "But personal influence is much diminished in bureaucracies. Our attitudes toward bureaucracies are connected to those involving authority. According to my theory, attitudes toward authority evolve from a traditional form, in which precedent is dominant. For examples, kings who pass on their authority to their children. At the second stage, we move to what I call a charismatic form, where personal characteristics of certain leaders are dominant. This focus on charisma helps overthrow traditional forms of authority, such as kings, but because charismatic authority is inherently unstable, a third form arises that I call rational and legal. This rational legal stage is essentially bureaucratic."

As he said this, Professor Weber seemed to collapse. His breathing became labored and his face was, suddenly, drained of all color. He slumped in his chair.

"Excuse me," he said, "but I . . . I simply cannot continue. Please forgive me. Perhaps we can continue this discussion at a later time. I don't know why but I simply don't have any energy. . . . I can't think . . . and when I consider how badly I have behaved and how I ruined the dinner party my dear wife organized . . . I am just . . . I don't know what to say. I'm just mortified."

"I'm a physician," I offered. "Can I be of any assistance? Do you need medical care?"

"No," he replied. "I don't feel well, but the cause is not physical. I am suffering, I should inform you, from terrible anguish. And I am very tired. Last night I spent many hours with Dr. Sigmund Freud, who is also here to address the conference and explain how his theory of psychoanalysis is involved in our hopes for social progress. He was kind enough to see me, to deal with matters that need not concern you. Now, what I need, more than anything else, is rest and quiet. I know my dear wife is worried about me . . . but I will be all right if I can get some rest."

"Of course," said Holmes. "We have no need to continue this interview at this time. Perhaps, when you have rested and are feeling better, you can come back and we can take up where our discussion left off, if that is necessary."

"Yes . . . anything you say," he said, weakly.

With that he slowly raised himself from the chair and with a measured pace left the room.

"A brilliant man, but a terribly sad one, Watson," said Holmes. "I have read several of his books and have been impressed by the breadth of his knowledge and the depth of his thought. But he is a tormented person. I think we might ask Dr. Freud to speak with us next. He spent some time with Weber last night and may be able to tell us something of interest about the good professor. Ask one of Lestrade's men to summon him, if you will."

"I'm looking forward to this," I replied. "I find Sigmund Freud's ideas interesting but they seem terribly far-fetched. Some people think he is a genius and others consider him a fraud. I truly look forward to meeting him so I can ask him about some of his notions."

"Controversial, no doubt," said Holmes. "I must confess, Watson, I find myself drawn to his theories, for reasons I cannot, at this moment, explain. I have read a number of his books . . . if you accept his premises, the conclusions follow logically. His insights into the human mind are, I think, remarkable. He would have made a brilliant detective. The good Dr. Freud is controversial, yes . . . but what if he's right?"

The contrast between Individual Psychology and Social or Group Psychology, which at first glance may seem to be full of significance, loses a great deal of its sharpness when it is examined more closely. It is true that Individual Psychology is concerned with the individual man and explores the paths by which he seeks to find satisfaction for his instincts; but only rarely and under certain exceptional conditions is Individual Psychology in a position to disregard the relations of this individual to others. In the individual's mental life someone else is invariably involved as a model, as an object, as a helper, as an opponent, and so from the very first Individual Psychology is at the same time Social Psychology as well. . . .

Group Psychology is therefore concerned with the individual man as a member of a race, of a nation, of a caste, of a profession, of an institution, or as a component part of a crowd of people who have been organized into a group at some particular time for some particular purpose.

Sigmund Freud, *Group Psychology and the Analysis of the Ego*. Quoted in John Rickman, ed. *A General Selection from the Works of Sigmund Freud* (169, 170).

chapter **seven**

FREUD EXPLAINED HIS THEORY OF GROUP PSYCHOLOGY

We were preparing to meet Sigmund Freud.

I must confess to a bit of unease about meeting him. I had read some of his works and was impressed by his knowledge and the power of his mind—or should I say, more properly, his imagination, since I found many of his ideas difficult to accept. Freud is a physician, like myself . . . but he seems to have abandoned the practice of medicine, as I understood it, for an investigation of the human mind. I did not know what to expect. You often have rather ridiculous notions about what an author whom you have read, but not met, is like.

"What's he like, Holmes?" I asked, nervously.

"You are in for a treat, my good Watson," said Holmes. "I have had the pleasure of meeting him a number of times . . . in the course of my investigations and for some personal reasons. Just relax and take comfort in knowing that Freud will always be five steps ahead of you in any discussion you might engage him in."

There was a knocking on the door. One of Lestrade's officers opened the door.

"Dr. Freud is here, gentlemen," he announced.

"Good," said Holmes. "Kindly show him in."

Sigmund Freud entered. He was much smaller than I thought he would be. He had a neatly trimmed beard and mustache, glasses with thick frames, and was smoking a long cigar.

Holmes got up and went to greet Freud. They shook hands.

"Ah, Dr. Freud. I have the great pleasure of seeing you again," he said.

Freud smiled enigmatically.

"It is good to see you again, Mr. Holmes," he said, in a soft, but firm voice.

"And this gentleman," Holmes said, turning to me, "is my trusty friend Dr. Watson. He has been of enormous service to me in many investigations."

I walked over and shook Freud's hand.

"Dr. Watson. It is a great pleasure to meet you," he said. "I have followed your activities in many of the cases in which you assisted Holmes. I always wondered what you might be like in person and now I have the opportunity and good fortune to find out. It is natural for people to wonder what people they read about or authors they read actually are like. We are, after all, curious animals."

I was astounded, I must say. It was as if Freud had been able to read my mind.

Freud took a seat. He looked very relaxed. There was what might be described as a light-hearted quality about him. His eyes had a brilliant gleam and his face had an animated and amused expression.

"I assume, Holmes, that you want to know about my conversation with Max Weber last night," he said.

"Yes," replied Holmes. "I don't know whether Professor Weber knows this, but yesterday I was engaged by his wife to prevent him from getting into trouble or from being harmed by someone else. He has received threats in Germany she said. I had made plans for Watson and myself to attend the party that Beatrice Webb is holding tonight . . . never thinking that Weber's wife would do something as foolhardy as arranging a dinner party for last night. I believe you were there. It was at that party that Lady Bracknell's diamond was stolen and that Weber and Durkheim got into an argument which led to Weber punching Durkheim."

"Yes, I was there," said Freud. "As Marianne Weber probably told you, one reason Weber came to the conference was to see me. He had written to me about the possibility of my treating him and we had made arrangements for me to see him last night. It turns out that he was in a much more agitated state than I had expected, though it was understandable, given the events that had just preceded it."

"I must say I sympathize with you," I replied enthusiastically. "I've had many patients who had similar experiences. It must have been terribly difficult for you."

"Difficult for me? Yes! But much more difficult for Professor Weber. We now have the police involved in a jewel robbery and we have the problem of the fight, if that's what we want to call it, between two world-famous sociologists. I went to Durkheim's room this morning and discovered he was not in. I inquired at the front desk at the hotel and found that his key was still in its box, so Durkheim, I take it, is missing. Perhaps something has happened to him, though I consider that unlikely. I cannot get too excited about a grown man, and a man who is well traveled, not occupying his hotel room one evening in a city like London. That, I must assume, is of secondary concern to you . . . it is, no doubt, because of the jewel robbery that you are here."

Holmes smiled.

"Quite remarkable, Dr. Freud. You are correct. My primary concern is to find Lady Bracknell's diamond and to restore it to her. The poor woman is terribly upset by its loss. But I also am concerned about the fact that Professor Durkheim has not returned to his room. It turns out that his wallet was found near the Thames and the police believe he might have been robbed and murdered, though I must say I have my reservations about whether Durkheim is, in fact, dead. People spend nights away from their hotel rooms for many different reasons."

"I agree with you," said Freud. "There are many possible explanations of his absence from his hotel room and why his wallet was found. He probably was robbed, but that isn't the same thing as being murdered. I'm sure he'll have a very good explanation for his absence when we see him next. But we are moving away from our subject. You wished to know what I learned from my discussion with Max Weber, and I will tell you."

"Good," said Holmes decidedly. "We still have to protect the professor from others who may wish to do him violence, and now, it seems, we must pay even more attention to protecting him from himself."

"We must differentiate depression from the way it is commonly used," said Freud. "It generally is used to suggest sadness, a feeling of despair and despondency . . . that kind of thing. In psychoanalytic thought, depression is a clinical syndrome that commonly involves difficulty in thinking, dejection, and weak psycho-motor activity. In depressed people, there is a decrease in concern about the outside world and an increase in self-criticism, a feeling of remorse and of guilt . . . which can be thought of as aggression against oneself. There is a great deal of anger in depression—which is directed toward oneself, but also can be directed outward. That helps explain why it was that Weber struck Professor Durkheim."

"I understand now," I said. "It is the anger in depressed people that can be directed outward, toward others, that explains Weber's unseemly behavior."

"Yes," replied Freud. "With severely depressed people, who don't respond to treatment, we always wonder whether they will kill themselves or kill someone else. Let me add something here. Depression is often caused by the loss of some loved person, what we psychologists call 'object loss,' but it is not the same thing, by any means, as mourning. The depressed person blames himself or herself for the loss of the loved one and this loss mobilizes repressed wishes of all kinds and all kinds of unconscious narcissistic self-mortifications. That is, terrible feelings of inadequacy and guilt, among other things.

"Now, as you know, Weber became depressed not very long after he had a fight with his father, who died a few weeks after the fight. Weber thus holds himself responsible for the death of his father and is also distraught about not having had the power to prevent this death. I trust you noticed that Professor Weber does not have much affect—that he moves slowly, that he is rather detached from others. That is to be expected. He is actually much improved over his situation in the years between 1897 and 1903, when he made a partial recovery. He has considerably improved in the years since then. He is now, I understand, able to deliver lectures and function as a professor, though it is with great difficulty.

"It seems likely that Weber strongly identified with his father. I learned last night, for instance, that he joined his father's dueling fraternity when he went off to the University of Heidelberg at the age of eighteen, where, like his father, he studied law. He also seems to have undergone a personality transformation and a physical transformation. He had been thin and reserved but at Heidelberg he became full bodied and a somewhat boisterous amoral hedonist. He was to change again, later, when he cast off his identification with his father and identified, instead, with an uncle.

"In addition, he had been engaged for a number of years to a cousin who was mentally disturbed, but eventually broke off that engagement. Then he courted another cousin, Marianne Schnitger, who had been seeing someone else. Weber stole her away from this man and married her in 1893. But he never consummated their marriage, and to this day has not been able to have sexual relations with a woman."

"Good Heavens," I sighed. "What a complicated person. I don't envy you this case. Not at all. I should not like to have to treat Professor Weber. Not at all!"

"Yes," he replied. "That is true. Complicated people, as you might imagine, often have many complexes."

With that he laughed. I was surprised by his ability to make light of what I thought was a terribly serious matter and frowned. Freud noticed my expression.

"Like anything else, Dr. Watson, you have to preserve your sense of humor despite the difficulties a particular case may cause. You must keep a certain distance and preserve a sense of objectivity, lest you be swallowed up by the power of this or that person's neuroses. Surgeons, as you no doubt know, often make jokes to help them keep up their courage. And so do we in the psychoanalytic movement. Humor is something we use to ward off anxiety."

"I can understand that," I replied. "I have often thought that it is Holmes's well developed sense of humor that enables him to carry on and deal with the many difficulties he faces as a consulting detective."

"Let me return to Weber," said Freud. "It seems that about five years ago, in 1904, Weber traveled to the United States and that experience seems to have made a considerable impression on him. It was there that he got his ideas about the importance of Protestant sects for the development of capitalism and of the importance of bureaucracies. He returned in a much better state, but still clinically depressed, and as a depressed person, full of anger that he generally directed against himself, but which he could also direct toward others. Thus, he was perfectly capable of attacking Durkheim, who is, I have been told, a most gentle and caring person. Now, of course, Professor Weber is consumed with guilt. He does not know that Professor Durkheim has not returned to his room. None of the others do either, I believe. Professor Weber thus is in a very delicate state and must be watched carefully, and protected from doing something rash—to someone else or to himself."

"By rash do you mean something like suicide?" asked Holmes.

"Precisely," said Freud. "Ironically, the subject on which Emile Durkheim has offered the most important sociological explanations. I'm afraid that Professor Weber is in some danger. He has, his wife informed me, received threats from others, but I fear he is a greater threat to himself. In addition, there is reason to believe that his finances are somewhat precarious. Given that state, it is conceivable, though highly unlikely, that Weber might have pocketed the diamond, if he saw it lying on the floor, and hidden it somewhere. This is possible, given his state, but I doubt that he could have done so—in part because he is a very rigid and highly moralistic person."

"I can understand your coming here to treat Weber," I said, "but what I don't understand is what you are doing at a conference full of sociologists and others involved with politics. I always thought your province was the individual mind, the human psyche."

Freud smiled.

"You must remember, Dr. Watson, that someone else is always involved in an individual's mental life as a model, a helper, or an opponent, so from the first, individual psychology is always, at the same time, social or group psychology. Remember I am always exploring the relation of an individual to others—his parents, his brothers and sisters, or the person he is in love with . . . that sort of thing. Group psychology is, therefore, concerned with the individual man as a member of a race, of a nation, of a caste, or a profession, or an institution, or as a component part of a crowd of people who have been organized into a group at some particular time for some definite purpose.

"My ideas about groups, let me add, have been influenced here by the work of a sociologist, Gustave Le Bon, whose ideas I find compelling. A group, as Le Bon explains, is extraordinarily credulous and open to influence, it has no critical faculty, and the improbable does not exist for it. It thinks essentially in images, which call one another up by association . . . just as they arise in individuals in states of free imagination. The agreement of these images with reality is never checked by any reasonable function. Groups always demand illusions and cannot live without them."

"Yes," I mused as he paused. "That makes good sense."

"I am glad that you find my argument persuasive," said Freud. "Now it is important to tie this group psychology to a topic related to individual psychology, namely the libido. I describe the libido as involving those instincts that have to do with everything that may be understood as involving the word 'love.' Essentially it involves sexual love and the desire for sexual union. But it also involves self-love, the love of one's parents, of one's wife, of one's children, friendship and love of humanity, in general. This love is, from my perspective, part of what I have called the 'group mind.' We find it, for example, in highly organized institutions such as the church and in the army, though it is generally hidden and members of these institutions wouldn't be aware of having such feelings.

"The evidence of psychoanalysis shows that almost every intimate emotional relation between two people which lasts for some time—marriage, friendship, the relations between parents and children—leaves a sediment of feelings of aversion and hostility, which have first to be eliminated by repression. The same thing happens when men come together in larger units."

"Aha!" said Holmes. "I can see how this might explain poor Professor Weber's plight."

"Yes, I'm sure you do," said Freud. "One can put two and two together. In my theory I suggest that identification is the earliest expression of an emotional tie with another person . . . what I have described to you earlier as, in psychoanalytic terms, an object. A little boy will exhibit a special interest in his father and will want to be like him and take his place everywhere. His father becomes the object of his identification. This has particular relevance to melancholia, an affection which counts among the most remarkable of its exciting causes and real or emotional loss of a loved object. A leading characteristic of these cases is a cruel self-depreciation of the ego combined with relentless self-criticism and bitter self-reproaches. That is what we find with Professor Weber, though he has improved greatly in recent years.

"Professor Weber, of course, is but one individual. But we often find groups of people, what I call primary groups, composed of a number of individuals who have substituted one and the same object for their ego ideal and have consequently identified themselves with one another. The intense emotional ties they have with one another might explain the lack of independence and initiative they feel. In other words, they develop what has been called the 'herd instinct,' though I find some fault with this notion because it does not leave room for the leader.

"In my lectures on this subject I have put forward a radical hypothesis, dealing with the myth of the father of the primal horde, which is at the very beginnings of society. He was exalted as the creator of the world because he had produced the sons who composed the first group. He was the ideal of each one of them, at once feared and honored, a fact which later led to the idea of taboo. These many individuals eventually banded themselves together, killed him, and cut him in pieces. None of the group of victors could take his place, or, if one of them did, the battles began afresh, until they understood that they must renounce their father's heritage. They then formed the totemistic community of brothers, all with equal rights and united by the totem prohibitions which were to preserve and to expiate the memory of the murder.

"Out of this group probably one individual was able to free himself from the group and take over the father's role. He justified his behavior by inventing the myth of the hero, who claimed to have acted alone in vanquishing the father, who was transformed into a totemic monster. Through this myth of the hero, some individual was able to emerge from control by the group psychology and become dominant.

"There is one other matter I should mention, here," continued Freud. "Human beings are, my theory suggests, naturally aggressive. Men are not gentle creatures who want to be loved, and who at the most can defend themselves if they are attacked; they are, on the contrary, creatures among whose instinctual endowments is to be reckoned a powerful share of aggressiveness. So the question arises—how does civilization inhibit this aggressiveness? *Homo homini lupus*—man is a wolf to man. What happens is that man's aggressiveness is introjected, internalized; it is sent back to where it came from, that is, it is directed toward his own ego.

"There it is taken over by a portion of the ego which sets itself over against the rest of the ego as the superego, and which now, in the form of 'conscience,' is ready to put into action against the ego the same harsh aggressiveness that the ego would like to satisfy upon other, extraneous individuals. Civilization, thereby obtains mastery of the individuals dangerous desire for aggression by weakening it and disarming it and by setting up an agency within him to watch over it like a garrison in a conquered city."

"You are correct in at least one respect," said Watson. "Your theory is, without question, quite remarkable. It is not one that I was familiar with . . . probably because I did not have the pleasure of attending your lectures on the matter. Man is a wolf to man, you say. I think I can agree with that. And I also find your metaphor about guilt being like a garrison in a conquered city most apt."

"You will be able to find a more complete elaboration of this theory in my forthcoming book, *Totem and Taboo*. It will be a compilation of four of my lectures on the subject," Freud said. "There is one other matter, that has some relevance to Professor Weber's case, that I might mention. And that is the matter of sublimation. You recall that I informed you that Weber has not been able to consummate his union with his wife, Marianne. Psychoanalytic theory can help explain this matter.

"There are, I have argued, a number of defense mechanisms which the ego uses to ward off anxiety, such as ambivalence, repression, regression, and, of particular interest here, sublimation. I would suggest that Professor Weber has sublimated, that is redirected or rechanneled his sexual drive into his writings, which explains why he has been able to be so productive as a scholar. You recall that I mentioned the church and the army as areas where sexual drives were inhibited and kept away from consciousness. In these institutions, and in countless others, we find the same matter of sublimation operating as individuals identify with one another by identifying with the same object, but repress, one way or another, their sexual desires. I might add that Weber is known to have had a very close relationship with his mother, suggesting certain Oedipal problems might also be behind his impotence . . . but I don't want to get into such a difficult area at this time."

"It is a great pity," Holmes said, "that you did not become a consulting detective, for you alone, among all men I know, would have rivaled me in this profession."

Freud was amused.

"But the work I do is very similar to what you do, Holmes," he said. "We are both interested in human motivation. You are concerned with criminals, whose behavior is shaped by many different forces, much of it tied to dark elements in their personalities and I am concerned with individuals, mostly neurotic, whose behavior is also shaped by their unconscious. I am referring to my notion that the psyche contains three elements: consciousness; a pre-conscious, of which we are only dimly aware; and the unconscious, which comprises the major part of the psyche and which is closed to us, due to the power of repression.

"I've also dealt with the psyche in my structural hypothesis, which posits a constant battle in which the ego tries to hold of two contending forces—the id, the representative of their drives which can be characterized as a cauldron of seething excitement, and the superego, our moral sensibilities. Criminals, for the most part, lack sufficient superego elements—their egos cannot control their ids, which dominate their behavior. My patients, many times, lack adequate id energy, for without an adequately developed id, a desire for pleasure, our egos are weak and our psyches are overly dominated by our superegos. The ego tries to help us adapt to the world and function in it, but if one or the other element of the psyche is too strong, you get—at the extreme—the criminal and the neurotic, and in some cases, both. That is, a criminal who is neurotic."

"Do you think the person who stole Lady Bracknell's diamond was criminal and neurotic?" Holmes probed.

Freud laughed in a good-natured way at the question.

"Most criminals are not very neurotic. They are, in many cases, fixated by a desire to have money, and they use means that we do not approve of to obtain the object of their desire. I do not know all the people who were at the dinner party well enough to be able to suggest which of them might have stolen the diamond, though I have met some of them before. None of them seems a likely candidate, but I cannot say, with any certainty, that one of them did not, somehow, in a moment of weakness, succumb to temptation. It is even conceivable that Lady Bracknell found a way, somehow, to steal her own diamond. If her finances were in desperate shape, the insurance payment on the diamond would be of great assistance. This scenario is not likely, but still quite possible, given how people can, at certain times, give in to the urges of their drives and do foolish things.

"Like you, Holmes, I am always on the lookout for clues that will help me solve the mystery of human behavior. You look for clues to crimes, missed by most others, which you use, along with your formidable powers of intellect, to solve crimes. What I do is not so different. I am always looking for clues to motivation and I find them in slips of the tongue, in references people make to others or to past experiences, to dreams—the royal road to the unconscious. No, Holmes . . . I'm much more like you than you give me credit for, except the crimes I try to solve are the crimes people commit against themselves and the subsequent torments they cause to their loved ones. We're both detectives, really!"

"Say what you will," declared Holmes, smiling. "I still say you'd have made a marvelous consulting detective. But we each must follow our destiny, and I would not wish to deprive the world of the contributions you have made . . . or are about to make. And, of course, you have helped countless people who you've treated."

"Helping patients? It's all transference," said Freud, laughing. "You are much too kind. But now I must work on my lecture to the group, so I will take leave of you and Dr. Watson, if you don't mind."

As Freud got up to leave, I walked over and shook his hand.

"I cannot tell you how much I enjoyed meeting you," I gushed like a much younger man. "I am, I confess, astounded by your ideas. But I will grant you that if one accepts your initial hypotheses, the consequences that follow do have a certain logic to them."

"Thank you, Dr. Watson" said Freud.

"I may have need to call upon you again," said Holmes. "I trust you would be willing, should some kind of emergency present itself."

"Most certainly," replied Freud. "I've had the pleasure of meeting Emile Durkheim before and look forward to meeting him again. We share, you no doubt know, an interest in suicide as well as other matters. But now I feel the need for a good cigar . . . and then I will return to writing my lecture."

"I've been fascinated by your work on symbols," I said. "Cigars seem to figure prominently in your thinking."

"Yes," replied Freud. "But you must remember—sometimes a cigar is only a cigar."

"Thank you," said Holmes, as Freud left the room.

"That man," added Holmes, "is a thinker of enormous importance. I think his ideas, though they deal with the human psyche, will be of great interest and utility to sociologists and others who study mankind."

It was unlike Holmes to be carried away like that, but Holmes was a superb judge of character and of intellect, and I had never known him to be mistaken in his evaluation of people we met. So I decided to investigate the work of Dr. Freud on my own when our work on this case was finished. Freud had said that man is a wolf toward man. I could agree with him on that, based on the many cases in which I had assisted Holmes.

Holmes took out his pipe, filled it with tobacco, and started smoking. "A good pipe and excellent tobacco . . . . they are very useful when you have to do some serious thinking. This case cuts deep, Watson. It cuts deep. But I believe I understand what has happened to Durkheim and I have an idea that might explain what happened to Lady Bracknell's diamond. We shall soon see whether my notions are correct."

The individual has become a mere cog in an enormous organization of things and powers which tear from his hands all progress, spirituality, and value in order to transform them from their subjective form into the form of a purely objective life. It needs merely to be pointed out that the metropolis is the genuine arena of this culture which outgrows all personal life. Here in buildings and educational institutions, in the wonders and comforts of space-conquering technology, in the formations of community life, and in the visible institutions of the state, is offered such an overwhelming fullness of crystallized and impersonalized spirit that the personality, so to speak, cannot maintain itself under its impact. On the one hand, life is made infinitely easy for the personality in that stimulations, interests, uses of time and consciousness are offered to it from all sides. They carry the person as if in a stream, and one needs hardly to swim for oneself. On the other hand, however, life is composed more and more of these impersonal contents and offerings which tend to displace the genuine personal colorations and incomparabilities. This results in the individual's summoning the utmost in uniqueness and particularization, in order to preserve his most personal core. He has to exaggerate this personal element in or to remain audible even to himself.

Georg Simmel, *The Metropolis and Mental Life*. Quoted in David Frisby and Mike Featherstone, eds., *Simmel on Culture* (184).

chapter eight

GEORG SIMMEL EXPLAINS
ACADEMIC POLITICS

The next professor we interviewed

was another scholar from Germany, Georg Simmel. I had never heard of the man but Holmes told me he was a person of much reputation in scholarly circles, with many unusual and interesting ideas. I had encountered enough unusual ideas with Freud to last me the morning . . . perhaps a lifetime, so meeting Professor Simmel was the last thing I wanted to do. But Holmes was steadfast.

"We must get to the bottom of all this," he reminded me. "And time is of the essence."

Simmel was a slender man with a neatly trimmed mustache and beard. He wore glasses and was dressed, I could surmise, in a handsomely tailored and expensive suit. Unlike Weber, who had shuffled into the room where we were interviewing people, Simmel walked in with a rather jaunty gait, smiling and seeming at ease.

"My name is Sherlock Holmes," Holmes said, and pointing to me he added, "and this gentleman is my dear friend and colleague Dr. Watson."

Simmel shook hands with us. His handshake was, I noticed, very firm . . . the handshake of a resolute person.

"Won't you have a chair?" said Holmes, pointing to the stuffed chair where Weber and Freud had sat.

"Ah, Mr. Holmes. . . . If only you were the rector of a university," Simmel said, laughing.

"Excuse me," I interjected. "But I don't understand the comment."

"Let me explain, Watson" said Holmes. "Professor Simmel is a thinker of the first rank, who has published many important books and articles. Yet he has not been offered a chair, that is a permanent professorship, at any German university because, I'm sorry to say this, these institutions have many anti-Semitic professors who have prevented him, because he is Jewish, from having a secure position. It is nothing less than a scandal."

"Yes, you are quite right," said Simmel, smiling. "I am and have been for many years an outsider. I was for many years a *Privatdozent*, an unpaid lecturer at the University of Berlin, dependent upon student fees . . . and later I was made an *Ausserordentlicher* professor there, a purely honorary position that didn't allow me to take part in university affairs. But, to be fair, there are other reasons as well, though they are much less important. My interests are so broad that many of the professors claimed I didn't belong in any discipline. I was, somehow, outside of the traditional disciplinary boundaries.

"And I am, it turns out, a very popular lecturer and many of my colleagues, whose candles, shall I say, do not burn very brightly, didn't relish my presence at the university. Mediocrity, I have often said, likes company—in universities and in all organizations. Max Weber, whose greatness is recognized by all, tried to get me professorships but was unable to do so. I do owe him a debt of gratitude for his efforts on my behalf. There are not many like him, unfortunately. We did found, with another professor, the German Society for Sociology, in an effort to help establish the discipline. I can call Max a friend but I cannot call him a colleague, alas.

"Fortunately, I am financially independent, so although I haven't received the honors I feel I deserve, it is not a critical matter. And not being a member of a department at a university may have freed me to do the kind of thinking and writing I've done—in part because I am an outsider and to many university scholars, perhaps even somewhat of a stranger.

"I am, you see, an ironist," he added. "I, who have done much, receive nothing from my university while many there, who have done nothing, receive much. I see life as ironic and ultimately comic. But I am certain that the scholars at the University of Berlin and the other German universities who have prevented me from obtaining a professorship all live with the knowledge, even though they may repress it, that they are persons of little importance who will leave nothing of any intellectual significance to future generations. They lead, for the most part, narrow, crabbed lives. They get their fulfillment by doing trivial work involved with helping run the university and keeping free spirits, like myself, out. My sense of confidence comes from the notion that my ideas and writings will have some lasting significance. I would like to found an institute to study everyday life and have applied to the Bracknell Foundation for funds to do so. That would be of some importance to my career . . . and to my theories."

I was astounded at the difference between Simmel and poor Professor Weber, who seemed so devoid of energy and so full of doubts about himself.

"I know very little about this new science of sociology, professor Simmel," I said. "Only what I heard from Professor Weber, who was here earlier. Is your work like his?"

"No, Dr. Watson, it is not," he replied. "We are all interested in the same thing—in human beings and the way they exist in society—but we go about studying it different ways. For example, some sociologists believe that society is like an organism and that you can use and adapt the methods of natural scientists to study society and focus on large, general laws about human behavior. Other sociologists argue that society is just an abstraction and that only individuals exist and that the actions of individuals are the subject of sociology. My view is somewhere in the middle. Saying that sociology is the master science that studies everything human beings do is self-defeating and much too ambitious. I see society as the name for individuals who interact with one another. Thus, the study of sociology is what might be called 'sociation,' the ways, the patterns, the forms that describe the way men associate with one another and interact with one another.

"Sociology asks what happens to us and by what rules people behave not insofar as they live their individual existences but insofar as they form groups and are shaped by their group memberships and their interaction within groups. I'm interested in the interactions among the smallest unit of society, individuals—but my focus is always on the interactions and the uniformities or forms to be found among different types of interactions. Thus, I am interested in various kinds of social types—the stranger, the renegade, the poor person. . . ."

"And we must not forget, of course," said Holmes, "the outsider."

"Yes, indeed," replied Simmel, laughing. "The outsider and his opposite, the insider. Concepts, we all recognize, have meaning only because they have opposites. One can only be an outsider if there are insiders just as we can't have poor unless there are rich. By your statement, Holmes, I discern that you are suggesting that there may be a strong, though hidden and perhaps disguised, autobiographical element to the work of sociologists."

Holmes smiled. "I have had conversations with eminent men who have implied as much. We cannot escape our pasts and we cannot escape our experiences, as much as we might try."

"Yes, yes," said Simmel, "that's correct. We are both individuals and social animals, at the same time. Man is not partly social and partly individual; rather, his existence is shaped by a fundamental unity, which cannot be accounted for in any other way than through the synthesis or coincidence of two logically contrasting determinations: man is both social link and being from himself, both product of society and life from an autonomous center. The individual helps determines society at the same time that society helps determine the individual. That is why sociology is so fascinating."

"But Professor Simmel," I interjected. "I can't see how you can have it both ways. Either society shapes the man or man shapes society. Something has to come first—either society or the individual."

"No, Dr. Watson, I must disagree with you here. There is a kind of reciprocal relationship at work in which individuals are shaped by societies, which they also help shape. In many actions, we find this reciprocal behavior, though it is often not easy to see. Consider the matter of rank—of those who are superior and those who are inferior in some organization or entity. Domination isn't simply a matter of power; what you find, if you look carefully, is that there is generally some kind of interchange between those who are superordinate and those who are subordinate. Often, those at the top of an organization are dependent, in various ways, on those who are beneath them in status and power.

"The individual, alas, has become a mere cog in an enormous organization of things and powers which tear from his hands all progress, spirituality, and value in order to transform them from their subjective form into the form of a purely objective life. It needs merely to be pointed out that the metropolis is the genuine arena of this culture which outgrows all personal life. Here in buildings and educational institutions, in the wonders and comforts of space-conquering technology, in the formations of community life, and in the visible institutions of the state, is offered such an overwhelming fullness of crystallized and impersonalized spirit that the personality, so to speak, cannot maintain itself under its impact.

"Of course, there are some things we can do . . . there is the fact that in modern societies a man may belong to many different organizations and while he may be dominant in some, he may be subordinate in others. The more groups a person belongs to, the more circles in which he moves, is an indicator of his level of cultural development. This is much different than in premodern societies in which people were members of few groups, such as trade guilds and kinship groups, and tightly controlled by them. Modern man has freedom, but with this freedom comes the danger of being overwhelmed and subjugated by the values found in modern societies. In one case, man has little freedom and in the other case, he might have too much. We are always torn between being attracted by various objects that we need for our cultural development and being dominated by them."

"Speaking of social interactions, a subject that is of consuming interest to you," said Holmes, "what can you tell me about the events that took place last night, when Lady Bracknell's diamond was stolen and when your friend Weber got into a fight with Emile Durkheim?"

"It was terribly distressing," replied Simmel. "I cannot explain what happened to Lady Bracknell's diamond. When Weber hit Durkheim, she fainted. A waiter was near her and grabbed her and prevented her from falling on the floor and seriously injuring herself. Everyone crowded around her. It was very chaotic. A minute or two later, Sigmund Freud examined her and found her well. Durkheim brought her some ice in a towel to help revive her. Then, a short while later, she realized her diamond was missing. We all searched for it but we couldn't find it. Her gold chain was on the floor but the diamond had been taken and, presumably, hidden somewhere. The police have scoured the restaurant but have been unable to find it. I can't believe any of the people who were at the dinner could sink low enough to take the diamond. The police have searched the cooks and the waiters and found nothing. So I am mystified. My notion about the importance of human interactions doesn't work very well when there is chaos and confusion.

"As for Max Weber, as I told you, he is a dear friend of mine, who tried many times to secure a professorship for me. So it was a terrible shock for me to see him strike poor Durkheim, who is much smaller than Weber and who seemed quite surprised by Weber's precipitous action. They had been having an animated discussion on Weber's notion of the significance of individual action in sociological theory and then, suddenly, Weber struck Durkheim. He, in turn, seemed mortified by the event and staggered out of the room where we had been dining. Until then, it had been a lovely evening."

"But if Weber was depressed," I asked Simmel, "how do you explain his hitting someone else? It doesn't make sense to me."

"Depressed people have little control over themselves, and while generally they are distant and full of self-reproach, they can, at times, act irrationally," Simmel replied. "Of course, we must recognize that had not Marianne arranged for the dinner, nothing would have happened."

"I imagine she did it to help cheer him up," I said. "Having a good meal with friends always lifts my spirits."

"Yes," said Simmel. "But there may be other aspects to the matter to be considered, from a microsociological perspective."

"What do you mean?" I asked. "Do you mean Weber's wife arranged to have the dinner party to make it possible for him to get in trouble? That she was hoping . . . if that's the correct word . . . that he would do something like that? I find it hard to believe," I said.

"Of course not," said Simmel. "But remember that one thing sociologists look for are hidden, latent, and covert aspects of human interactions. From a microsociological perspective, when dealing with what I call 'dyads,' we find complicated relationships between men and women, husbands and wives, along the lines of domination and submission and power relationships. Marianne probably thought that the party would be good for her husband, but nevertheless you must admit that she subjected him to a risk that he could not deal with successfully."

"But why?" I asked.

"It's hard to say," Simmel replied. "People are not aware of the real reasons they do many things. If they were, there would be no need for a science of sociology. Or any of the social sciences. No, it is because people do not, or cannot, or don't want to, understand why they behave the way they do in their many different social interactions that explains why sociology is so important. Have you not wondered why it was that Marianne, who is a lovely woman whom I adore, organized this dinner party when she knew that her husband was in danger and was a danger to himself and to others? You have met with Max Weber and heard about his many troubles. His psychological troubles are rooted in his family history but also, I would add, in his relationship with Marianne. She loves him, but she may also at times, without being aware of what she is doing, help him in various ways to undermine himself."

"That makes sense to me," said Holmes. "I have found, in many cases that I have been involved with, that victims often find ways to assist those who victimize them. It is the tangled web that we weave as we live our daily lives that must be untangled. We think we see clearly ahead, but from your perspective, we are also blind to what we do and the real motives behind what we do. Weber's wife couldn't have anticipated that he would get into an animated discussion about social theory with Durkheim and that would lead to Weber's striking Durkheim, but organizing that dinner party was, most certainly, for poor Weber, a terrible thing."

"And for Durkheim, as well," replied Simmel. "There were, we must remember, not one but two victims of Marianne Weber's foolishness—her husband and Emile Durkheim. I have not seen him today. I trust he was not seriously injured. He may, however, feel it necessary to avoid others, due to a sense of humiliation. Or he may not be feeling well. Would you happen to know?"

"No, we do not know yet how Professor Durkheim is," replied Holmes. "But we should know soon, and with luck, he will be at the party that Mrs. Webb has organized for tonight."

"I certainly hope so," said Simmel. "That would be a great comfort."

"I have no other questions to ask," said Holmes.

"Since you have no other questions, I would like to return to my dear wife, who is waiting for me."

"Of course," agreed Holmes. "I cannot let you go without telling you how interesting I find your ideas. This morning has been, without question, the most intellectually stimulating and challenging morning I've had in years. And it is not even time for lunch."

"Thank you," replied Simmel. "Perhaps, Mr. Holmes, you are somewhat of an outsider, too . . . like myself. I know that you are a person of great reputation, with remarkable powers of observation and inference. It is too bad that you have not chosen to be a sociologist, for the profession would greatly benefit from a person of your great intelligence and astuteness. You might want to consider this an invitation."

"From one outsider to another," replied Holmes. "But what would the insiders have to say about the matter?"

Simmel laughed. When he had left I turned to Holmes.

"Durkheim at the party tonight? For all we know, the poor man was killed last night," I said.

"No, Watson . . . I seriously doubt that Durkheim is dead. But we shall find out soon enough. We are having quite a morning, Watson. I have found it enormously interesting and, I hope, useful. But I know, from past experience, that you must be very hungry by now."

I glanced at my watch.

"It is coming on ten o'clock, Holmes, and I would dearly love to have my breakfast. Claridge's has a marvelous breakfast spread and I propose we interrupt these interviews for a short while and have something to eat. I was only able to have a cup of tea and some toast before your message arrived."

"A capital idea, Watson," said Holmes. "I would like to have something to eat myself. Let us have some breakfast and then we can return to our labors with renewed vigor."

"And now we must prepare for our next interview."

"And who will that be, Holmes?" I asked.

"None other than the infamous Russian revolutionary figure, Vladimir Lenin," said Holmes. "If you will kindly ask one of Lestrade's men to fetch Lenin in about an hour, I would most grateful."

I got up and stuck my head out into the hallway, where one of Lestrade's detectives was stationed.

"Holmes would like to interview Lenin in an hour," I told him, then turned back around to face Holmes. My good friend was deep in thought.

"Let's have breakfast," he said as if struggling to understand something. "I confess, Watson, that I too, am hungry."

"Simmel said something about wanting to start an institute to further his work . . . and having applied to Lady Bracknell's foundation for funds to do so," I reminded him. "Do you think he might have pocketed the diamond and hid it? He strikes me as a very clever man."

"Too clever, I would imagine, to do something as stupid as that," replied Holmes. "Though you never know what people will do when confronted with an opportunity to realize their ambitions. I doubt that he is our jewel thief, but until we've interviewed everyone, we cannot be sure."

The exploiting classes need political rule in order to maintain exploitation, *i.e.*, in the selfish interest of an insignificant minority, and against the vast majority of the people. The exploited classes need political rule in order completely to abolish all exploitation, *i.e.*, in the interests of the vast majority of people, and against the insignificant minority consisting of the slave-owners of modern times— the landowners and the capitalists. . . .

The overthrow of bourgeois rule can be accomplished only by the proletariat, as the particular class, which, by the economic conditions of its existence, is being prepared for this work and is provided with the opportunity and the power to perform it. . . . The doctrine of the class struggle, as applied by Marx to the question of the state and of the Socialist revolution, leads inevitably to the recognition of the *political rule* of the proletariat, of its dictatorship, *i.e.*, of a power shared with none and relying directly upon the armed force of the masses. The overthrow of the bourgeoisie is realisable only by the transformation of the proletariat into the *ruling class*, able to crush the inevitable and desperate resistance of the bourgeoisie, and to organise, for the new economic order, *all* the toiling and exploited masses.

Vladimir Lenin, *State and Revolution* (22).

chapter nine

THERE WILL, FOR A SHORT
PERIOD, BE A DICTATORSHIP
OF THE PROLETARIAT...

The last sitting for breakfast

at Claridge's was at ten o'clock, though I'm sure we could have procured something to eat later, due to the many debts the directors of the hotel owed to Holmes for his services over the years. When the manager of Claridge's, Vittorio Settembrini, saw us approaching the dining room, he scurried over and led us to a table.

"We're pleased to offer you and your colleague Dr. Watson breakfast, with our compliments," he said, beckoning a waiter to serve us. Satisfied with the waiter's response, the manager bustled off again, apparently caught up with another one of the hotel's million problems.

I looked around the room. The sideboard held china teapots, ready for Chinese and Indian tea, and pots of coffee in glistening silver pitchers. Next to the pots were plates of scones and toast and multicolored jars of marmalade, jams, and honey. On another sideboard I was thrilled to notice a row of silver dishes full of poached eggs, bacon, sausages, ham, kidneys, haddock, and salmon. A third sideboard offered various cold meats—pressed beef, tongue, ham, pheasant, grouse, and partridge. Nearby were many hothouse fruits—melons, nectarines, peaches, strawberries, raspberries.

"We shan't go hungry, Holmes," I said eagerly, as I surveyed all the foods that we could choose. I must confess that, after a long morning of thinking, I felt very hungry.

"No, not at all, Watson."

Holmes turned to the waiter.

"I would like some coffee and a small pitcher of cream, a plate with some melon, scones and raspberry jam, two scrambled eggs, and four rashers of bacon," he said. "That should be more than adequate. And what of you, Watson?"

"I would like some ham, some pheasant, poached eggs, and toast. I will have some black tea and cream, also."

"Thank you," said the waiter, who raced off. Several minutes later, some young men with large trays appeared next to our table and the waiter served us what we had ordered.

"I was upset when your message came and I wasn't able to have a proper breakfast, but this more than makes up for it. You can't beat Claridge's for good food."

"And we're saving a small fortune," Holmes replied, "thanks to the largesse of the manager. This is a very expensive hotel. I find it somewhat strange that the conference is being held here, but I guess the scholars and writers who will be giving talks like their comfort. One can believe in social progress all the more if one is living in luxury."

"Come now, Holmes," I replied. "The speakers are persons of some consequence. You wouldn't expect them to accept living in poor quarters, and the conference is an event that will attract much attention. Where else but Claridge's, I ask."

The food was quite delicious. I ate ravenously, I must admit, while Holmes just picked at his food.

"Perhaps," said Holmes. "We are next to interview Vladimir Lenin, the self-appointed, some would suggest, champion of the working classes. Does it not strike you as odd that he would be staying in a hotel frequented by people who are very wealthy—aristocrats, millionaire businessmen . . . that sort of people."

"Not at all," I replied, "since his way is being paid for by the sponsors of the conference. No doubt he could not afford to stay here were that not the case. People are seldom reluctant to spend other people's money. I may not be a sociologist, but that is one law of society that I would be willing to propose."

Holmes laughed.

"I fear that this morning's associations with social theorists is doing terrible harm to you, my dear Watson," he said. "You are already proposing theories and laws after only the briefest contact with sociologists. By tonight, you may well be quite impossible."

While we were dining, a striking looking man, younger than us, came over and asked whether he might join our table.

"I had just finished my breakfast," he said, "when I noticed you sitting here. It is my understanding that you are the famous detective Mr. Sherlock Holmes. And this man," he added, pointing to me, "is your colleague Dr. Watson. I believe you are interviewing all the people who were at the dinner party last night."

"You are correct," Holmes said.

"My name is Vladimir Lenin," he said.

I had seen photographs of Lenin in the press, but they didn't capture his presence. When he had sat down to join us, I felt in the presence of a powerful personality, a man with enormous energy and willpower. He was bald, and had a large forehead, a large nose, and thick lips. There was something of the Tartar in his visage. He also had bushy eyebrows, a mustache, and a neatly trimmed and pointed beard. His eyes were probably his most prominent feature—they were small, deep-set, and had a piercing quality to them. He was wearing a dark suit of some rough material.

"Thank you, sir, for being kind enough to submit to this interview," said Holmes.

"I have had much experience with the police," replied Lenin, calmly. "At least I am confident that whatever happens this morning, you won't be turning me over to the police. That doesn't happen in England . . . at least I hope not!" With that he laughed. "I found the events of the dinner party last night most interesting— a jewel robbery, in the best traditions of bourgeois criminality, and a violent assault on an unsuspecting victim. I must confess that although I didn't steal Lady Bracknell's diamond, I have some sympathy with the person who did so—driven to a dangerous act by the imperatives of a bourgeois capitalist society. The exploiting classes need political rule in order to maintain exploitation, i.e., in the selfish interest of an insignificant minority, and against the vast majority of the people. So it is only natural that, from time to time, we find instances of personal rebellion against this terrible domination . . . which may take the form of stealing a useless jewel from a very rich person."

"You need not fear the police from this little talk we are about to have . . . or anything, for that matter," Holmes said. "Would you be good enough to tell us what you can about events that transpired at the dinner party last night."

"Very little of consequence," replied Lenin. "We had a very nice dinner and I was chatting with Beatrice Webb when we were disturbed by the voices of Max Weber and Emile Durkheim, who were having an animated discussion and had started shouting at each other. Durkheim was pointing a finger at Weber, as if to make some point. I don't know why, but for some reason Weber suddenly struck Durkheim in the face. His nose started dripping copious amounts of blood, which he tried to stop with a large handkerchief. When this happened, Lady Bracknell fainted and everyone raced to help her. Shortly after she had revived, Freud went to see if she was all right. The next thing we knew, her diamond was gone. The police came and searched everyone and looked around the restaurant, but they couldn't find the jewel. The party broke up shortly after that incident. We were told to remain at the hotel so we could be interrogated the next morning. That's as much as I can tell you."

"Have you any idea about who may have stolen this gem?" asked Holmes. "It is a very valuable jewel, worth a great deal of money."

"I'm sure you'll find a way to blame it on some member of the working class—the cook, one of the waiters . . . someone like that. You'll argue that the eminent scholars who were at the dinner party would never stoop to such a thing—while, in fact, any one of them might have taken Lady Bracknell's diamond and found some clever place to hide it. It is always the working class that is blamed for all such criminal matters, while the bourgeoisie that enslaves them talks endlessly about abstractions like morality and justice. One might argue that in an unjust society, it is the elites, the upper classes, who are the real criminals, but their criminality is carried out on such a grand scale that they are revered as heroes and statesmen. Those who steal a few shillings and are caught are locked in jail and those who steal millions from the poor are looked upon as great men. It is a big farce!"

"I see," said Holmes. He took out a cigarette and lit it. "Given your beliefs, I would like to find out what you are doing at this conference, since your notions about sociologists and bourgeois societies, such as we find in England, are so strong."

"True," said Lenin. "But I am very much concerned with the matter of social progress. In fact, I have devoted my life to the matter."

"I have read your book *What is to be Done?*," said Holmes, "which I found most stimulating. I trust you were invited here mainly to deal with political considerations, as the panelists and speakers consider the question of social progress."

"Yes," said Lenin. "That is correct. I have, over the years, been in contact with Sidney and Beatrice Webb and have, in fact, translated their book *Industrial Democracy* into Russian. That was a number of years ago. I'm currently living in Paris so it was not a great inconvenience to come to London, to give a lecture at the conference and to spend some time with the Webbs. It was in London, it so happens, that Marx did much of his research and writing, so it is a city that means a great deal to me and others in my movement."

"You know," I interjected, "when I was a young physician, I treated Marx for some minor ailment. So, by chance, I have met two of the more important Communist thinkers. A remarkable coincidence."

"Yes, I am a Communist," replied Lenin. "I'm afraid the other speakers at this conference will not appreciate some of the comments I am about to make. At our dinner party last night, for instance, I noticed that among the people there, only Beatrice Webb and myself had written very much on politics. I have recently published a book, *Materialism and Empiriocriticism,* which explains my ideas on politics. All the others at the party were sociologists. And sociology, to my mind, is a petty bourgeois field of inquiry. Will society ever make much progress if it has to wait for the ameliorations to be brought by champions of the status quo, like Max Weber, who spend their time investigating bureaucracies and other matters of little consequence?

"Marx's philosophy is, first and foremost, a revolutionary philosophy. It argues that class differences are basic in any society and that the workers, the proletariat, those who have nothing to sell but their labor, will never escape from wage slavery and domination, if they have to wait for sociologists to document their degrading lives . . . or pettifogging bourgeois politicians or labor union leaders.

"Marx argued that the history of all hitherto existing society is the history of class struggles. Freeman and slave, lord and serf, guild-master and journeyman, in a word oppressor and oppressed stood in constant opposition to one another, carried on an uninterrupted, now hidden, now open fight that each time ended either in a revolutionary reconstitution of society at large or in the common ruin of the contending classes. It is my intention, to the extent that I am able, to help the revolutionary forces struggling for the oppressed masses gain power.

"I used the term 'materialism' in the title of my book because Marxism is a materialist philosophy. It argues that it is the economic relations that exist in a country that shape the consciousness of the proletariat. The mode of production of material life, Marx believed, determines the general character of the social, political, and spiritual processes of life. It is not the consciousness of men that determines their beings, but, on the contrary, their social being determines their consciousness."

"Marx's theory, then, is just the opposite of Weber's," Holmes said. "He seems to believe, if I followed his argument correctly, when he was discussing his theories just a while ago, that ideas shape society."

Lenin smiled.

"You are correct in setting Weber against Marx," he replied. "Weber is a bourgeois idealist, with his head in the skies. Had I been here when he was discussing his theories, I would have asked him where these ideas come from. What generates ideas? Marx argued that men are the producers of their conceptions and ideas— real, active men, as they are conditioned by the development of the productive forces in which they live. . . . And what is important here is that the productive or economic forces, the base, shapes their consciousness, that is the superstructure. The institutions of society are basically reflections of the base, the economic conditions that pertain in a given society.

"They are based upon ideas that the ruling class, which controls the newspapers and other means of transmitting ideas, wants them to have. That is why Marx argues that the ideas of the ruling class are, in every age, the ruling ideas—that is, the class which is the dominant material force in society is always, at the same time, the dominant intellectual force. And what the ruling classes want the working classes, the proletariat, to have is a false consciousness of their situation and their possibilities . . . so they will not rise up in arms and throw out those who torment them.

"In so doing, they will escape from the *alienation* that consumes them. For most workers, the work is external to the worker, it is not part of his nature, which means he does not fulfill himself in his work but denies himself, has a feeling of misery not of well-being. His work is not voluntary but imposed, forced labor. It is not the satisfaction of a need but only a means of satisfying other needs. The basic one being the need for a wage to feed himself and his family, but in capitalist societies, the proletariat is beaten down. In such societies every man speculates upon creating a new need in another in order to force him to a new sacrifice . . . everyone tries to establish over others an alien power in order to find there the satisfaction of his own egoistic need."

"You've painted a very grim picture," I said. "As I think about my own life, I don't have those feelings you have been discussing. My life is pretty comfortable and I'm quite satisfied with my station in life and my possibilities."

"Of course you do, Dr. Watson," said Lenin.

I could see he was beginning to become animated. His eyes gleamed with intensity.

"Because you are, though you may not realize it, a member of the ruling class. In Marxist terms, you are a member of the petit-bourgeoisie, a segment of society that serves the ruling classes. Your well-being, from a Marxist perspective, has been purchased at great cost, however. . . . I am talking of the many members of the working classes, or what we call the proletariat, who toil long hours for little more than starvation wages. Forgive me for saying so, because I do not want to insult you sir, but your well-being and sense of comfort is tied to your class and your occupation. If you were a collier or a laborer in a factory working long hours for a pittance I doubt that you would feel the way you do."

At this point Holmes entered the conversation.

"Tell me," Holmes said, "if class shapes consciousness, why is it that people from wealthy classes become revolutionaries? Why aren't the Webbs apologists for capitalists? Why aren't you? And why is it that some members of the working class are so conservative?"

"You've asked the right question," said Lenin.

"Let me answer the second part of your question first. Remember, Marx argued that the ideas of the ruling class are always the ideas of the masses. It is normal, then, to expect that members of the proletariat have illusions about themselves and their possibilities. So these people are to be expected to accept the views of the ruling class.

"The first part of your question is more difficult. Let me suggest that there are always some who, because of their experiences or their personalities or some other accidents of history, are improperly indoctrinated by the ruling classes. They form the vanguard of the revolution and find that they have to fight not only those who form the ruling classes but also the proletariat, which has become degraded and which accepts the ideas of the ruling class."

"And what, may I ask," said Holmes, "is your contribution to socialist—or should I call it Marxist—theory. Do you see yourself as, in essence, a spokesman for the theory or have you added to it in some way. I have read Marx, and find him very provocative. One cannot help but sympathize with his sense of outrage over the terrible suffering of the working classes, but I always end

up wondering where it leads. You have said that sociologists and
their theories have little impact on the world. Has Marx? Will he?"

"You must remember, Mr. Holmes, that Marx died less than
thirty years ago," replied Lenin. The fire in his eyes was burning
brightly. "But in those years his ideas have had enormous influence. There are some within our movement, the Mensheviks, who
believe that Russia will evolve, gradually, into some kind of a social
democracy and there will not be a need for a revolution. The
Communist movement that I am aligned with, the Bolsheviks, argues just the opposite. Given the unprecedented circumstances
that occur in Russia, we believe that revolution will not occur in
industrialized societies like England or Germany, as Marx pre-
dicted, but in less developed agrarian ones, such as Russia. While
it is always possible, of course, that a well-developed capitalist society can evolve into socialism, we Bolsheviks believe that feudal
societies can also give birth to socialism—if there is a severe crisis
that facilitates this change. That notion is, perhaps, my most important contribution to revolutionary socialist theory to date.

"In order to be successful, Communists must be highly organized, with a centralized structure. The revolution needs men
who are committed totally to it, and who are willing to use violence as a political weapon. We believe that the end justifies the
means, and if we need violence to bring forth a society in which
the masses will be able to avoid the exploitation that they have
suffered, then so be it.

"Until now the capitalist nations have been able to hold off
the triumph of socialism by exporting their problems to lesser developed colonial nations. With the immense profits they make
from exploiting backward people, they can pay higher wages at
home and, by buying off the working classes, put off revolution for
a while. But this imperialist stage of capitalism will only lead to a
war amongst the competing capitalist nations and thus will facili-

tate the creation of a classless socialist society, characterized, as Marx put it, to each according to his need and from each according to his ability.

"Marx believed that the emancipation of the working class is the work of the working class itself, and we Communists exist only to help the working class. The working class, on its own, can only develop a trade-union consciousness. It may realize the necessity of combining in unions to fight against employers and to work to get the government to pass necessary labor legislation. But it cannot develop a revolutionary ideology by itself. It needs the intellectuals in the Communist Party to guide it toward revolution and freedom.

"There will be, for a short period, a dictatorship of the proletariat, to guide the development of a new worker's state. In this new state, all property will belong to the workers, and with this, class differences will be eliminated, leading to the end of history, since history is the study of class conflict. The dictatorship of the proletariat will hold down the exploiting class and prevent a counterrevolution and it must organize a new social and economic order. This dictatorship is necessary because the proletariat, after years of suffering, is not fully class conscious. This new democratic state will exercise the strictest control over labor and consumption, and by the systematic use of violence it will lead to a higher form of democracy than the venal and rotten parliamentarism of bourgeois society."

"You have offered an eloquent and passionate, but in many ways disturbing, explanation of your views," said Holmes. "And though I am not as much of a student of social thought as I should be, in part because I have crimes to investigate, I cannot help but be disturbed by what seems to be a logical contradiction—the idea of your setting up a dictatorship in the name of the working classes. Marx argued that the state will wither away. I have my doubts about this dictatorship you mention withering away and giving up its power voluntarily. I make this case based on what I know of human nature and what I've read by psychologists and sociologists."

"But you must realize, Holmes," Lenin said, "scientific impartiality is neither possible nor desirable. Social philosophy is the means by which parties use ideas to engage in class struggle. This so-called scientific detachment we are supposed to find in our economists and philosophers is only a mask covering their role in maintaining the status quo in the bourgeois societies where they are employed. These bourgeois social scientists are instruments of the ruling classes and work to give members of the proletariat illusions. Proletarian social science is different. . . . It represents the future, and is tied to the inevitable triumph of Communism.

"This is what I will say at the conference on social progress. Bourgeois economists and sociologists merely talk about social progress; we in the Communist movement plan on doing something to bring about true social progress."

"I hope you are correct about bringing true social progress," said Holmes. "By the way . . . is it possible that you took Lady Bracknell's diamond so as to help finance your movement? Would that be a concrete step to further social progress?"

Lenin laughed. "No, I did not take the jewel, but if I could have, I probably would have done so. I cannot regard appropriating a large diamond from a wealthy old lady as theft, you must understand. I would classify it as an incident in the war between the classes that would enable the wealthy finally, even though not voluntarily, to do something of value for the poor.

"I am certain about my ideas," he continued, "and certain that my movement will, one day, be triumphant. Whether I am alive to see it is another matter," added Lenin. "If you have no further questions, I would like to leave and take a walk. I have to work on my address to this congress."

"Thank you, sir," said Holmes. "I appreciate your being so forthcoming with us . . . and for telling us what you remembered of the party."

When he had left, Holmes turned to me.

"What do you make of Lenin?" he asked.

"He has about him the air of a zealot," I replied. "His ideas are, to my mind, wild and unrealistic, but he considers them to be absolutely true."

"Yes, Watson, you are correct about Lenin," said Holmes. "But I would use stronger language. Lenin is a fanatic . . . very much like the kinds of fanatics one finds holding certain religious beliefs. And it strikes me that these Communists are fanatics as well and that Marxism has as much the character of a religion as of a political philosophy. Weber would probably say the same thing. I think this Lenin is a very dangerous man, and being highly intelligent and possessed of enormous willpower, he may yet make a name for himself. If, God forbid, there ever is a dictatorship of the proletariat in Russia, as he thinks there will be, I certainly would not like to be subject to him. Zealots like him are fully capable of murdering thousands, if not millions, to achieve their goals. Mark my words, if there is a revolution in Russia that succeeds, and I fear that is likely to happen when the Communists come to power, the land will be drenched with blood in the name of human progress."

Amid all crouched the freed slave, bewildered between friend and foe. He had emerged from slavery—not the worst slavery in the world, not a slavery that made all life unbearable, rather a slavery that had here and there something of kindliness, fidelity, and happiness—but withal slavery, which, so far as human aspiration and desert were concerned, classed the black man and the ox together. And the Negro knew full well that, whatever their deeper convictions may have been, Southern men had fought with desperate energy to perpetuate this slavery under which the black masses, with half-articulate thought, had writhed and shivered. They welcomed freedom with a cry. They shrank from the master who still strove for their chains; they fled to the friends that had freed them, even though those friends stood ready to use them as a club for driving the recalcitrant South back into loyalty. So the cleft between the white and black South grew. Idle to say it never should have been; it was as inevitable as its results were pitiable. Curiously incongruous elements were left arrayed against each other—the North, the government, the carpet-bagger, and the slave, here; and there, all the South that was white, whether gentleman or vagabond, honest man or rascal, lawless murderer or martyr to duty.

W. E. B. Du Bois, *The Souls of Black Folk* (21).

chapter **ten**

The famous black American social thinker

and advocate W. E. B. Du Bois was the next person we interviewed. He was a handsome man who had been well educated in the United States . . . at Harvard, the foremost university there, so I had learned from reading about him in the newspapers. He had a stately bearing and was, at the time, a man who looked as if he were of around forty years of age. After Holmes introduced himself and me to the good professor, he sat down.

"You were at the dinner party last night, so I understand," began Holmes.

"Yes, I was," replied Du Bois, in the straightforward American style. "It was a very fine evening, with many important thinkers. At the dinner party were men and women of the highest attainments in the development of social theory . . . until it was prematurely ended by the unfortunate altercation between Max Weber and Emile Durkheim and the jewel robbery."

"Did you see what happened?" asked Holmes.

"I did not," said Du Bois. "I was deep in discussion with Georg Simmel when I heard a bit of shouting, and by the time I turned my head to see what was happening, Weber had, so it seems, struck poor Emile Durkheim. He was holding a handkerchief to his nose, which was bleeding copiously. He seemed terribly distraught.

There was a commotion when Lady Bracknell fainted. Shortly after she regained consciousness, she discovered her jewel was missing. Then the police came and searched everyone—I found that most humiliating, though I understand why it was necessary. I cannot understand who among the dinner guests could have stolen her diamond. We found the chain but someone obviously tore the diamond from the chain and hid it somewhere in the restaurant. But the police could not find it. I found the evening most unsettling, Mr. Holmes. Most unsettling. I hope that Professor Durkheim was not seriously hurt."

"I do not believe so," replied Holmes. "I understand that he took a walk after the dinner party broke up and did not return to his room last night, so the police are quite concerned about where he might be, but I am not worried."

"I hope you are right," said Du Bois. "Durkheim is a very fine person, in addition to being a sociologist of the highest abilities. He is the father of French sociology and a thinker who has had enormous influence. I have found his books of major importance and would suggest that, in many respects, we have common interests."

"Is that so," said Holmes. "Could you kindly explain these common interests."

"With great pleasure, sir," said Du Bois. "We are both interested in the question of social progress and what are the major impediments to this progress. He has suggested that the division of labor leads to what he called organic societies—those characterized by weak links between people and the breakdown of a sense of community. My approach is that there is another great division among people that needs to be dealt with—namely the problem of racism.

"The great problem of the twentieth century is the problem of the color line. You must remember that the world is supported to a larger and larger degree by products from a continent like Africa, and governed by the industrial caste which owns Africa. It seems clear to me that the masses of men within and without civilization are depressed, ignorant, and poor chiefly because they have never had a chance, because the results of their labor have been taken from them.

"For centuries the world has sought to rationalize this condition and to pretend that civilized nations and cultured classes are the result of inherent and hereditary gifts rather than climate, geography, and happy accident. But now we are beginning to see a decline of European culture. The possibility of this has long been foreseen and emphasized by the socialists, culminating in the magnificent and apostolic fervor of Karl Marx and the communists; but it is hindered and it may be fatally hindered today by the relations of white Europe to darker Asia and darkest Africa, by the persistent determination, in spite of the logic of facts and the teaching of science, to keep the majority of people in slavish subjugation to the white race."

"So it is *race* that you see as the fundamental cause of conflict among men," I said. "And not class."

"You are quite correct, Dr. Watson," he replied. "But you must remember that class is also important. Poverty is unnecessary and the clear result of greed and muddle. There was a time when it was due mainly to scarcity, but today it is due to monopoly founded on our industrial organization. This strangle hold must be broken. It can be broken not so much by violence and revolution, which is only the outward distortion of an inner fact, but by the ancient cardinal virtues of individual prudence, courage, temperance, and justice and the more modern values of faith, hope, and love."

"We have just had a discussion with Vladimir Lenin," said Holmes. "I do not think he would be willing to wait for faith, hope, and love to change societies around. He argued that violence was needed to set up a dictatorship of the proletariat, as he put it."

"I cannot agree with him, though I recognize he is a thinker of some consequence. The proletariat of the world consists not simply of white European and American workers but overwhelmingly of the dark workers of Asia, Africa, the islands of the sea, and South and Central America. These are the ones who are supporting a superstructure of wealth, luxury, and extravagance. It is the rise of these peoples that will lead to the rise of the world. Indeed, one phase of this color problem led to the Civil War in my nation. The question of Negro slavery was, I believe, the real cause for this war."

"But I must confess that I find your argument, except for your disdain for violence, much like his. He told us not more than an hour ago about his theory of imperialism and the way the capitalists were able to export their problems to just the people you have been discussing."

"We are similar in our belief that the peoples in the non-European worlds have been terribly exploited and are still being exploited," he said, "but I do not see violence as a way for these people to better themselves. I have faith in the power of freedom and democracy to lead these peoples to higher levels of economic development and spiritual progress. I see race, not class, as the fundamental cause of the problems societies have faced over the centuries.

"In my own life I can remember the difficulties I faced, as a youngster, by race. Something happened to me one day and it dawned upon me, with a certain crudeness, that I was different from others and was shut out from the world by a vast veil. That difference, of course, was my black skin. I had, thereafter, no desire to tear down that veil and attempt to creep through. I held all beyond it in common contempt. As years passed, this contempt began to fade and the worlds I longed for, and all their dazzling opportunities, were theirs, not mine. But they should not keep these prizes, I said. Some, maybe all, I would wrest from them. Just how I would do it I could never decide. With other black boys the strife was not so fiercely sunny: their youth shrunk into tasteless sycophancy, or into the silent hatred of the pale world about them and mocking distrust of everything white or wasted itself in a bitter cry—'Why did God make me an outcast and a stranger in my own house?'

"You see, the Negro is a sort of seventh son, born with a veil and gifted with second-sight in our American world—a world which yields him no true self-consciousness but only lets him see himself through the revelation of the other world. It is a peculiar sensation, this double consciousness, this sense of always looking at one's self through the eyes of others, of measuring one's soul by the tape of a world that looks on in amused contempt and pity. One ever feels his twoness—an American, a Negro. That is one of the problems all black people in America must wrestle with. But I think we can overcome it."

"I find it very curious," said Holmes, "but I can almost imagine the problem you have just mentioned, in your very moving account of your early days, as something said by Professor Simmel."

"That is most perceptive," replied Du Bois. "You see, he is very much interested in the problem of the stranger, so there are certain things we both have in common. I am a black man and he is a Jew. We are both, despite the difference in our skin colors, very much alike . . . in that in America and Europe we are almost always forced by others to be strangers. It is not a stance we wish to take but we cannot avoid it."

"I can understand that," said Holmes. "I would imagine that your ideas will be of great interest to the organizers of this conference on social progress. For I can see that you genuinely believe it is possible."

"Not only possible, Mr. Holmes," said Du Bois, "but inevitable."

"If you can provide us with no other information on the lamentable conclusion to the dinner party last night, you are free to go," said Holmes.

"Thank you," he replied. "I do not have any idea who might have taken Lady Bracknell's diamond. I cannot believe it was one of us, one of the people who were at the most excellent dinner, and the search by the police suggests as much. But everyone was searched and the room was searched and the diamond is missing. Someone must have thought up a most ingenious way to hide that gem. This person should get high marks for ingenuity and a very low mark for morality."

He got up and left the room.

"A most impressive man, Holmes," I said.

"And a valiant fighter for his people," Holmes replied. "He is a man of enormous dignity and valor."

Society is not all the illogical or a-logical, incoherent and fantastic being which has too often been considered. Quite on the contrary, the collective consciousness is the highest form of psychic life, since it is the consciousness of consciousnesses. Being placed outside of and above individual and local contingencies, it sees things only in their permanent and essential aspects, which it crystallizes into communicable ideas. At the same time that it seems from above, it sees farther; at every moment of time it embraces all known reality; that is why it alone can furnish the minds with the moulds which are applicable to the totality of things and which make it possible to think of them.

Emile Durkheim, *Moral Education* (9).

chapter eleven

What strikes me is that each of our scholars seems to have different opinions as to what the basic problems we face are and how they should be resolved.

WATSON IS PUZZLED BY THE CONFLICTING THEORIES OF THE SOCIAL THINKERS

We were surprised by a knock on the door.

A waiter entered the room carrying a large tray.

"The manager sent you some tea and sandwiches," he said. He placed the tray with the tea, the sandwiches, and some small cakes on a table.

"Thank you," I said. "I had a lovely breakfast, but I must say that I was beginning to feel, ever so slightly, the pangs of hunger."

I poured myself some tea and started eating a sandwich.

"Watson," said Holmes. "Your appetite amazes me, though I also could use something to eat. These discussions with the social thinkers we have met have been, in a way, quite arduous."

I poured him some tea and placed a ham sandwich on a plate and passed them to him. He started eating his sandwich.

"What strikes me," I replied, "is that each of our scholars seems to have different opinions as to what the basic problems we face are and how they should be resolved. For example, the Frenchman Durkheim suggested that the division of labor was the primary cause of our social problems, leading to anomie and the breakdown of a sense of community and other difficulties. Then the German sociologist Weber suggested that ascetic Protestantism was behind the development of capitalism which, in turn, shaped our society and values. He also argued that bureaucracy was the dominant force in society and implied, if I understood him correctly, that authority has moved from those with charisma to the bureaucratic form and now to what he called a rational-legal form of authority."

"Yes," said Holmes. "Each person we talked with has a different theory and each of the theories makes sense, too. Our theorists are all brilliant men and women, but they are also human beings and susceptible to all the different physical and psychological problems humans must endure."

"Freud, of course, argues that the human psyche is the primary thing to keep in mind and that man's aggressive nature is only contained by guilt, so we are all like prisoners in a conquered city kept in check by our own consciences. He also dealt with the social dimension of his thought. But no sooner had Freud left than another German sociologist, Georg Simmel, came and suggested that human interactions are the basic element in society and that we are both individuals, with our own ideas, but also social animals, imbued with values and beliefs from our social situation. At lunch, Lenin said that class differences are the most important consideration, and that unlike Weber, who stressed the importance of ideas, the economic system is basic, for it generates beliefs, values, and institutions that are sympathetic to the beliefs of the ruling classes. Now Professor Du Bois enters the picture and tells us that race is the fundamental problem we face and that progress is based on solving the race problem."

"Yes, you are correct," said Holmes. "Of course you have suggested that it may be the structure of the brain that is of major significance and that matters involving the cerebral cortex may be behind criminality and impulsive behavior. And next, Watson, I am confident that we will find yet another theory that explains why society has not progressed and what must be done. All of these thinkers here are devoting their lives to understanding why people act the way they do, and they are all, in a sense, carrying on a great dialogue with one another about their subject—a dialogue about which they are passionate and deeply involved. When you have minds as formidable as we have in our speakers, you can expect very interesting, and in some cases provocative, ideas to come forth.

"We have but one more person to interrogate, the remarkable Beatrice Potter Webb. I have followed her career in the papers, for she and her husband, Sidney Webb, are a couple much in the news for the last twenty years. They are very prominent political activists and social reformers and she has written books on matters such as the cooperative movement and the trade union movement in Britain. The Webbs also founded the London School of Economics among other things. They were also in the Fabian society with George Bernard Shaw and H. G. Wells. She knows just about everyone worth knowing in the political world. A most interesting woman."

"She was a very beautiful woman when she was young," I said. "Very beautiful. I must confess that I was quite surprised when she married Sidney Webb. One wouldn't imagine that she would find him a suitable mate, but I take it they have had a happy marriage. They've been married almost twenty years now. How the time flies."

"Now that we have had a light repast, I suggest you inform Lestrade's minion that we would like to see Mrs. Webb. She was asked to come and make herself available this morning, even though she lives in the city."

The fact that someone is poor does not mean that he belongs to the specific social category of the "poor.". . . It is only from the moment that [the poor] are assisted . . . that they become part of a group characterized by poverty. The group does not remain united by interaction among its members, but by the collective attitude which society as a whole adopts toward it. . . . Poverty cannot be defined in itself as a quantitative state, but only in terms of the social reaction resulting from a specific situation. . . . Poverty is a unique sociological phenomenon: a number of individuals who, out of a purely individual fate, occupy a specific organic position within the whole; but this position is not determined by this fate and condition, but rather by the fact that others . . . attempt to correct this condition.

Georg Simmel, "The Poor."

chapter **twelve**

I became convinced That one must remedy The social order to help people, and not expect Them to pull Themselves up by Their own boot straps

BEATRICE POTTER WEBB EXPLAINS HER SOCIAL PHILOSOPHY TO HOLMES

One of Lestrade's men

opened the door and announced, "Gentlemen . . . Mrs. Webb is here," as she entered the room. She had an air of assurance about her, probably because she had done so much public speaking. She, and her husband, Sidney, knew all the most important people of the day.

I remembered, perhaps a little frivolously given the circumstance, how beautiful she had been when she was young; now, in her fifties, she had matured into a very handsome woman. I wondered how it is that some beautiful women marry men who do not match them, in any way, in physical attractiveness, but that, I realized, was probably a foolish idea on my part, because I have a male's point of view.

"Good morning, gentlemen," she said, walking into the room and disturbing my reverie. She spied the chair she was to sit in and walked over to it and sat down without waiting to be asked.

"Now," she said briskly, "how may I help you?"

Holmes was the first to reply.

"My name is Sherlock Holmes," he said, "and the gentleman sitting beside me is my colleague Dr. Watson."

"I am pleased to meet you," she said with a gracious smile. "Over the years I have followed, with great interest and admiration, your exploits as a consulting detective. I've always thought it was a pity that a man of your intellectual abilities, Mr. Holmes, didn't go into politics. Had you done so, there is no question in my mind but that you would have become prime minister . . . and a very excellent one, too."

"You flatter me," replied Holmes. "I have left the realm of politics to others. In that endeavor, I have noticed that you and your husband have made many important contributions."

Mrs. Webb smiled again, this time with a humorous expression on her face.

"I trust you are interested in what transpired at the dinner party that Marianne Weber organized last night," she said.

"Yes," encouraged Holmes.

"I can say very little. I know that Marianne thought it would be pleasant for the main speakers at the forthcoming conference to dine together and so arranged for everyone to attend a dinner party. I am having a party tonight, as you no doubt know, but for a larger group of people. I've invited the main speakers and also a number of political luminaries and a number of writers who are friends of mine.

"In any case, the dinner last night had gone well and it was just ending when Max Weber and Emile Durkheim became involved in a discussion of their theories. Weber insisted that the individual and his actions were the basic atoms of sociology, while Durkheim attacked this notion as simplistic and suggested, rather strongly, that social phenomena are basic and are the true subject matter of sociology. That, in turn, seems to have led to an argument and then Max suddenly punched Emile in the face.

"We were all shocked. Emile, poor man, seemed dazed by the blow to his cheek. His nose started bleeding copiously, so he took a handkerchief to stem the flow of blood. We were about to go and minister to him when my friend Cecily Bracknell uttered a loud shriek and fainted, dead away. A waiter caught her, fortunately, before she fell to the floor and injured herself. We all rushed to her side. Emile rushed into the kitchen to fetch her a glass of ice water. In the confusion, it seems that someone took Cecily's diamond and secreted it away somewhere in the dining room or the kitchen. That is all I can tell you. It all happened very quickly. I have no idea who might have taken it. The people who were at dinner cannot be suspected and the waiter, poor fellow, is terrified that the blame, somehow, will fall upon him."

"Perhaps he hopes, in the near future, not to be so poor?" murmured Holmes. "Kindly tell me, do you have any idea why Professor Weber acted so rashly?"

"I was not party to the conversation and don't know what Emile might have said to Max that might have led to his becoming violent. Of course, violence is the way men often attempt to resolve problems they have."

"Unfortunately, you are correct," I agreed.

"Perhaps, if I tell you something about my background, you will understand my reasons for becoming involved in politics. I was the eighth daughter of a wealthy merchant, Richard Potter. My mother eventually gave birth to a son but he died when just a baby. Being a woman, I received relatively little formal education, so I was forced to educate myself, with the help of my governess. I read a great deal and was particularly interested in science and philosophy. My mother regarded me as the only ungifted child in the family. When my mother died I was quite young and remained to help take care of my father. He was friends with the famous social philosopher Herbert Spencer and my meeting him was of great consequence.

"When I was older I met and fell in love with Joseph Chamberlain, but we differed greatly in our personalities and so the relationship ended, quite bitterly, alas. I then became interested in doing charity work. My father died and left me 1,000 pounds a year, which helped support me while I did research on a book on the cooperative movement in Great Britain. I became convinced that one must remedy the political order to help poor people, and not expect them to pull themselves up by their own bootstraps. It was the structure of society that was at fault, not the individual. My researches in the East End of London, where there is terrible poverty, convinced me of this. Around this time I was introduced to Sidney Webb, a member of the Fabian Society. We married several years later in 1892 and have had a joyous marriage, working together, tirelessly, for the improvement of society."

"I take it," I said, "that you are comfortable with your role as a writer and a public speaker. I understand that you are much in demand in the latter respect."

"Actually, Dr. Watson, when I started addressing audiences I was quite petrified. But when I felt inclined to be timid, as I was going into a room full of people, I always would say to myself, 'You're the cleverest member of one of the cleverest families in the cleverest class of the cleverest nation in the world, so why should you be frightened?' And that gave me great comfort. And now I am quite used to speaking to large audiences, especially about the problems of women. You are no doubt aware that I have become, in recent years, part of the women's movement here in England."

"Yes," said Holmes. "I have read that you had, for a long time, opposed giving the vote to women."

"That is true," she admitted. "At one time, in earlier years, I was against granting the electoral franchise to women, but I have changed my mind. My objection to granting the vote to women was based, for the most part, in my disbelief in the validity of any so-called abstract rights, whether to votes or to property. I see life as a series of obligations—of the individual to the community and of the community to the individual) I didn't believe that women, as women, were under any particular obligation to take part in the conduct of government. I thought women might be content to leave the rough and tumble of politics to mankind, with the object of concentrating all their energies on what seemed to me to be their peculiar social obligations—the bearing of children, the advancement of learning, and the handing on from generation to generation of an appreciation of the spiritual life."

"And what caused you to change your opinion?" I asked. I could see that Beatrice Webb was a formidable person, with great presence and confidence and a keen mind. Still, I was more inclined to agree with her earlier opinions on the issue of women voters.

"This division of labor I alluded to works only if men and women feel that government is acting as their common agent. What I had thought of as the main preoccupation of women quickly became the preoccupations of the community as a whole, and this meant that women must fulfill their functions by sharing the control of the state in those directions. It has been necessary, alas, to manifest our beliefs in unconstitutional forms, via the persistent interruptions of public meetings and other breaches of the peace. But we are driven to such actions by not having the constitutional methods of asserting our views. That is why I believe women must be given the vote, whether married or single, propertied or wage earning. That is the only way we can achieve justice and have our rights protected."

"So you think the disruptions of the suffragettes are morally valid," suggested Holmes.

"I most certainly do," she replied firmly. "I have devoted my life to securing justice for the working classes and I believe that women are not being treated justly, and as we have no recourse to traditional political means to achieve our ends, we must use our ability to disrupt day-to-day activities as a means of attracting attention to our cause and ultimately gaining the vote."

"I should say, at this point, that I agree with you on this matter," Holmes interrupted. "If we are to be a true democracy here in England, it is only fitting that women be given the vote."

I must confess that I was somewhat surprised by Holmes's radical views. Of course, in our long friendship we had not had much occasion to discuss politics or social philosophy, being preoccupied with foiling criminals and bringing them to justice.

"Let me offer an anecdote that might be of interest in regards to my connection with women's rights." Mrs. Webb became animated as she told her story. "A man once said to me 'I think all this talk about feminism is nonsense. Any woman would rather be beautiful than clever.' I replied, 'Quite true, but that is because so many men are stupid and so few are blind.'"

I found Mrs. Webb's story most amusing, and so did Holmes, who laughed more heartily than I have seen him do in years.

"One last thing. In your conversations last night with Professor Durkheim, did he say anything about friends he might have in London, from whom he might be gaining solace or with whom he may be staying?"

"No," she reflected, "he did not. He has been to London many times, he informed me, but he said nothing about friends to whom he might repair. Is there something wrong, perchance?"

"Yes," replied Holmes, "he is missing since last night, but I am not really worried about him."

"That gives me great comfort," she replied. "Since you have met all of the featured speakers, and are deeply involved in the matter of Professor Durkheim's disappearance, I'd like to invite both of you to the party I am giving tonight. I hope you will accept my invitation and that you will find a way to bring him with you."

"Yes, of course we will," assured Holmes. "And thank you for being kind enough to invite us to your party. It will be a pleasure to see some of the scholars we've interrogated in a more relaxed atmosphere."

"Very good," she said, with finality.

At that, Beatrice Webb got up and left the room.

"I would not want to lock horns with that woman," said Holmes. "She is extremely intelligent and not easy to best. The women's movement has a great champion in her. I do not think it would be profitable for us to speak with Weber's wife again, so that means we have interviewed everyone who was at the dinner party last night. That being the case, Watson, let us find whether the good professor has returned and claimed his key."

But a god is not merely an authority on whom we depend; it is a force upon which our strength relies. The man who has obeyed his god and who for this reason, believes the god is with him, approaches the world with confidence and with the feeling of increased energy. Likewise, social action does not confine itself to demanding sacrifices, privations, and efforts from us. For the collective force is not entirely outside of us; it does not act upon us wholly from without; but rather, since society cannot exist except in and through individual consciousness, this force must also penetrate us and organize itself within us; it thus becomes an integral part of our being and by that very fact this is elevated and magnified.

In the midst of an assembly animated by a common passion, we become susceptible to acts and sentiments of which we are incapable when reduced to our own forces; and when the assembly is dissolved and when, finding ourselves alone again, we fall back to our ordinary level, we are then able to measure the height to which we have been raised above ourselves.

Emile Durkheim,
Elementary Forms of
Religious Life (240).

chapter **thirteen**

THE GOD THAT HOLDS YOU OVER THE PIT OF HELL, MUCH AS ONE HOLDS A SPIDER OR SOME LOATHSOME INSECT OVER A FIRE...

We left the room

where we had interrogated the people who were at the party and walked over to the front desk of the hotel.

"Has Professor Durkheim returned, by chance?" asked Holmes.

The clerk looked at the keys of people who were out and told us that his key was still there and that he had not returned.

"I suspected that would be the case," said Holmes, a trifle too mysteriously for me. I turned, ready to ask why he had been making such insinuations all day.

It was just at that moment that a very tired looking Emile Durkheim walked into the lobby of Claridge's.

"Mr. Holmes and Dr. Watson," he greeted us. "I have had a most extraordinary evening, and have gathered information of the most remarkable kind. I had high hopes for research into the role of religion in the life of London's poor people, but my wildest hopes have been surpassed. At the price of some physical discomfort, however."

"Good to see you, Professor Durkheim," said Holmes, clearly unperturbed. "Quite a few people are worried about you. If you will forgive me, I must send a message to Scotland Yard. It will only take a moment."

I tried to hide my surprise, both at the Professor's return and Holmes's cool reaction to it.

Holmes brushed past Durkheim, stumbled, and clutched the professor's sleeve. I began to worry about my old friend's health. Certainly, I would not want to grab at that grimy jacket without a good reason for doing so. Holmes quickly regained his balance, however, and continued toward a nearby policeman. A message passed between them. Then the policeman raced off and Holmes returned to where I was standing with Professor Durkheim.

"Lestrade will come," Holmes told me under his breath, fidgeting with the handkerchief in his own jacket pocket.

"I am most interested in hearing about your adventures last night," Holmes said. "But perhaps it would be good to wait for you to go to your room to freshen up. Watson and I will wait for you in the lounge."

"Yes, I could use a good wash and a fresh shirt. Then I will be happy to join you and tell you of my London adventures." With that, he got his keys and went up to his room.

Holmes and I went to the lounge where we had a brandy. At the table next to us, Lenin and Du Bois were having a discussion.

"Don't you see," said Du Bois, gesturing in the American manner, "that your revolution and the dictatorship of the proletariat that you hope to create will lead . . . must lead . . . inevitably to tyranny? It is only through democratic means that a society can become just. Once a dictatorship becomes established—whether it is in the name of the people or not—it will be impossible to get rid of it. The state can never wither away, as Marx said it would."

"If we wait for democratic means," replied Lenin, "we will never achieve a just and free society. The proletariat are not democratic by nature, having been debased by decades of bourgeois control and manipulation, and one cannot get a government that will be able to sustain itself, for the welfare of the people, without a violent revolution and the leadership of a small group of dedicated people who will rule in the name of the people. There is no other way."

They continued their discussion for some time, each arguing that his approach was the correct one and trying to persuade the other man to change his mind.

When Durkheim had taken his greatly desired bath, and was refreshed, he joined us and recounted his adventures.

"You must remember, gentlemen," he said, "that I am a scholar and have spent much of my life teaching students at my university, doing research, conducting experiments, looking for books in libraries and, above all, writing. I spend most of my time in my study, writing books. I have not had the opportunity to spend as much time as I would like with the working classes and those who are commonly described as being in the lower orders in Paris and most certainly not in London."

"The life of a professor, as you describe it, seems terribly narrow and proscribed," said Holmes. I thought of our own experiences, traveling across all levels of London society.

"It is. . . . It is, indeed," replied Durkheim. "In a strange way, it is quite monastic. I have written a great deal about religion. Indeed, what will be one of my major works, which I will call *The Elementary Forms of the Religious Life,* is devoted to that subject. But I had never thought that my life, and the life of most of my colleagues, I must add, was so highly structured and so narrow. But my passion for social theory, and for explaining man's relation to his fellow man in this world, I now realize, is very similar to the passion religious people have for theology, and explaining, as best they can, man's relation to God in the next world."

"How do you explain that?" I questioned him. "I must confess to being naïve about the scholarly life, but how is it that professors get so caught up in their work that they hardly know anything about life. Quite ironic, that you who would explain social life to others have no social life of your own, to speak of."

"There is something fascinating about sociological theory," replied Durkheim. As he spoke, he patted his pockets like a man looking for a tobacco tin. A worried look passed briefly over his face, as he clutched at his pocket. Throughout this performance, however, his voice remained calm.

"It takes control of you and leads you on, for you feel that your ideas, and your ideas alone, are adequate to explain social relations among men. You convince yourself that you have not made the mistakes of others, and so you spend your life developing your theories and attacking the theories of those who do not agree with you. There is something intoxicating about abstract thought, which helps explain why there have been so many philosophers and theologians . . . and sociologists, too, of course."

"I take it that last night was of some consequence for you," said Holmes, bringing him back to the subject at hand.

"Indeed it was," enthused Durkheim, "for I mingled with the working classes and was able to see, firsthand, how they lived. Or, to be more correct, how some in London live. I doubt that they are much different from those in other cities in England. As I mentioned, after we had been searched by the police to see whether we had stolen Lady Bracknell's diamond, and the dinner party broke up, I suffered a severe nosebleed and attempted to stop it with a large handkerchief that I was carrying. I also secured a piece of ice from the kitchen to minimize the swelling that I feared would occur, and holding that piece of ice with a napkin which a cook was kind enough to give me, I left the hotel. What was worse, however, was that I was slightly dizzy, and so I wandered out of the hotel, thinking some fresh air might be beneficial. I had intended to do some research on the role of religion in the lives of London's poor and decided to do so that evening. I found myself wandering around London. After a while, I discovered that I was lost and hadn't the slightest idea of where I was. But the streets were much meaner than others I had seen in London. The fog seemed more polluted, and the men and women looked burdened by more than just the bundles they carried. I had, I realized, wandered into a section of London where the poor lived.

"The streets were crowded and a number of people, some of whom seemed to be intoxicated, jostled me.

"It occurred to me that I might benefit from something to drink to calm myself and help me gather my wits. I came upon a public house and went in. It was crowded with people from the lower orders. I went to a bench and sat down there.

"'What'll you have, love?' asked the barmaid.

"'A brandy, thank you,' I said.

"'Very good,' she said. She poured a brandy and brought it to me.

"'You don't look well,' she said. 'Are you all right? Can I do anything for you?'

"'I've had a slight accident,' I said. 'But I shall be fine.'

"'You're a foreigner,' she said. 'It's best not to linger here too long. The regulars here don't like foreigners and really don't like people from the upper classes. I can tell from your clothes that you're a gentleman. You shouldn't come to places like this, if you know what's good for you.'

"'Thank you, thank you,' I said, and paid her.

"'I'll keep an eye on you while you're here and make sure you don't come to harm,' she added.

"Although it was odd to be protected by a woman like her, I was grateful. I drank my brandy quickly and left the establishment. As I was walking I was accosted by two roughs. One of them came up to me and pulled out a knife. He told me he wanted my wallet and no harm would come to me if I didn't resist or cry out. I gave him my wallet and then the two men disappeared down a dark alley.

"At one corner I came upon a large room that was brightly lit. In it, men of all sorts, though most were in rough clothing, were singing hymns. As I walked by, a woman in a uniform—I believe I had stumbled upon a Salvation Army meeting—noticed I was unsteady and came to assist me.

"'Won't you come in and rest for a few moments, poor soul,' she said to me.

"She guided me into the room and brought me to a chair in the back of the room, where I sat down. It was a large room full of long tables that extended almost from wall to wall, with just a narrow aisle on either end. The people in the room finished their singing and sat down. In the front of the room, one of her colleagues, a man of about forty, with a grim look on his face, started speaking to the assemblage."

You are all sinners, he said, and if you do not reform and give yourselves to God, if you do not give up your drink and abandon your loose ways, you all will come to a bad end and roast in hell for a million, million years. The bow of God's wrath is bent and the arrow made ready on the string and justice bends the arrow at your heart, and strains the bow, and it is nothing but the mere pleasure of God, and that of an angry God, without any promise or obligation at all, that keeps the arrow one moment from being made drunk with your blood. The God that holds you over the pit of hell, much as one holds a spider or some loathsome insect over the fire, abhors you and is dreadfully provoked. His wrath towards you burns like fire. He looks upon you at worth of nothing else but to cast into the fire. He is of purer eyes than to bear to have you in his sight. You are ten thousand times so abominable in his eyes as the most hateful and venomous serpent is in ours. O sinners . . . consider the fearful danger you are in. 'Tis a great furnace of wrath, a wide and bottomless pit, full of the fire of wrath, that you are held over in the hand of that God whose wrath is provoked and incensed as much against you as against many of the damned in hell. You hang by a slender thread with the flames of divine wrath flashing about it, and ready every moment to singe it and burn it asunder.

"At this, the seated people all started crying and lamenting. I thought I might be carried away by a flood of tears. The poor souls, as the woman called them. They were, I could see, simple men with simple minds. 'Save me, save me,' one man shrieked. 'I give myself to you from this day on. No more drink, Lord, and no more wenching . . .' and there were many others who spoke out in a similar manner. There was much crying and pleading and praying. Some of the men were wearing bowlers and others cloth caps. Everyone was in a disheveled state, with rough clothes, and many, I could see, from the way they stood, wobbling and unsteady, were suffering from drink. So that was it. The woman on the sidewalk who guided me into this meeting thought I was a drunk, like so many of the others in the room.

"Meanwhile, the speaker was droning on, cataloguing, in great detail, the endless torments that awaited these poor souls if they did not reform and give themselves to the Lord.

"'Will you not stay for some food?' she asked.

"'Why thank you,' I said. For some reason, I had become quite hungry. 'I have been robbed,' I said, 'and have no money to give you. I have a room at a hotel but have no way to get there.'

"'You need not have any money,' the good woman assured me. 'And you may stay with us the night. Tomorrow morning we will feed you and return you to your hotel. Do you need medical care? Are you ill?' she asked.

"'No, no thank you,' I said. 'I have had an accident and hurt my nose. I am slightly dizzy . . . but not drunk. You may be assured of that.'

"A short while later that evening, she led me to a dormitory where I slept the night in a deep sleep. The next morning, I woke late and after the people at the missionary hostel fed me, they arranged for someone to deliver me back to this hotel."

"Extraordinary," I said. "I have read about these Salvation Army meetings but never had occasion to attend one. That image of people hanging on a slim thread over a bottomless fiery pit . . . quite remarkable." My own adventures slowed after I stopped living with Holmes.

"Remarkable, yes," replied Durkheim. "In the research I have been conducting on religion, I have found that people in assemblies such as the one I attended can behave in remarkable ways and the power of religious leaders to stir people's passions in such assemblies is incredible. But events like prayer meetings must be held often and regularly to strengthen the sentiments which are aroused, since they will abate if not constantly reinforced. I have gained some valuable insights from my researches about our need for being with others who have things in common with us in gatherings, and about the power of collectivities . . . especially of the religious kind. We are social animals but much of our social nature is tied, I believe, to religious organizations of one sort or another, which help us assuage our loneliness and counter tendencies toward anomie and alienation."

"That seems quite reasonable," I replied.

"And what of the jewel that was stolen? Has that matter been resolved?" asked Durkheim. The question seemed little more than a formality.

"Soon," said Holmes. "This evening, at the party, I will solve the mystery of where Lady Bracknell's jewel has been secreted. You may be able to help me."

"I'll be happy to do whatever I can," replied Durkheim, looking worried.

"Yes," said Holmes mysteriously. "I'm sure you will."

Inasmuch as adornment usually is also an object of considerable value, it is a synthesis of the individual's having and being: it thus transforms mere possession into the sensuous and emphatic perceivability of the individual himself. This is not true of ordinary dress which, neither in respect of having nor being, strikes one as an individual particularity; only the fancy dress, and above all, jewels, which gather the personality's value and significance or radiation as if in a focal point, allow the mere *having* of the person to become a visible quality of its *being*. And this is not, not *although* adornment is something "superfluous," but precisely *because* it is.

Georg Simmel,
"Adornment."

chapter **fourteen**

You put me through this terrible anxioty as an experiment?

MAX WEBER PUNCHES EMILE DURKHEIM IN THE FACE.

Beatrice Webb's party at Claridge's

was just getting started. Waiters were bringing champagne to the guests, carefully avoiding the policemen stationed around the room. Holmes and I joined Mrs. Webb, her husband, Sidney, Sigmund Freud, and Lady Bracknell.

"I feel that this conference will not do justice to the rights of women," Beatrice Webb was saying. "If you look at the list of speakers, most of them are men. Women, alas, are terribly under-represented, and I have the great burden of trying to make those interested in social progress to consider the needs of women—in all lands, in all social classes. For whether we are in an advanced nation, like England, or in a more backward land, women are, everywhere, exploited and treated unfairly. When I think of myself and how foolish I was about the matter of women having political power, I realize how difficult it is for women and for men to realize the importance of this matter."

Freud smiled and muttered to me, "What do women want?" He said nothing loud enough for Mrs. Webb to hear, considering the delicate situation.

"Ladies and gentlemen," interrupted Holmes, rapping on a wineglass with a knife to gain everyone's attention. "I was asked by

Inspector Lestrade of Scotland Yard to investigate the matter of Lady Bracknell's missing diamond. I am now, at this moment, prepared to solve the mystery."

Conversation stopped and the expectant sociologists turned toward Holmes. Durkheim was the only one who did not look hopeful at Holmes's announcement.

Holmes reached into his pocket and took out a small package wrapped in his handkerchief. He unwrapped it, and there in his hand, sparkling brilliantly in the light, was Lady Bracknell's diamond. I was no less surprised than the others. I was with Holmes all day. When did he find the diamond?

"Thank you so much, Mr. Holmes," gasped Lady Bracknell. "But where . . . where was the diamond and how did you find it?"

Holmes smiled indulgently.

"Really, it's quite simple. To understand what has happened, I must tell you about something that happened two nights ago. I was visited by Professor Durkheim, who was worried about Professor Weber. It seems that Professor Durkheim feared that Professor Weber was in danger of doing something rash—to someone else or to himself. At that time, he also gave me a letter and asked me not to open it until he gave me word to do so.

"While not opening, the letter, I examined it. By feel, I could tell it was a single page of good stationary, not a bundle of documents. As I spoke to Durkheim, I held the envelope up to the table lamp, in order to read through the envelope. Even you, Watson, who knows me so well—even you thought I was merely being absent-minded.

"But still, why did Durkheim instruct me not to open the letter, when he could easily have someone deliver it later? When Durkheim disappeared, I realized what he meant. The disappearance was a sign that I should open the letter. I did so while I was waiting for Watson to arrive.

"In it was a description of an experiment he had in mind, to see how the various sociologists and social thinkers would respond to some provocation he planned. Let me read it to you.

My dear Mr. Holmes:

It is my intention to conduct a small experiment, so to speak, with my colleagues who will be giving presentations at the conference on social progress here in London. I intend to provoke some kind of an argument with one of the speakers and force the other speakers to react. Most of my colleagues at this conference have written a great deal about theoretical matters of sociological interest, and yet I wonder whether they have much experience, in the real world, with many of the topics they deal with in their writings. I fear not and wonder whether they, like myself, have done most of their work in their book-lined studies. It is my intention to rectify this sociological unworldliness, so to speak, and force my colleagues to determine how their theoretical positions affect their responses to the events that transpired.

I hope that this little experiment will not cause undue distress to any of my fellow speakers and I apologize, beforehand, for any anxiety or discomfort I may cause any of them. I hope to bring my colleagues down from the lofty abstractions in which they espouse their theories and force them to see, with their own eyes, how they respond to something that happens to them . . . to bring them down, if only for a short while, from the clouds of theory into the real world.

Emile Durkheim

"I take it he had in mind provoking an argument with Professor Weber or Professor Simmel or perhaps even Dr. Freud over some matter of sociological concern. Durkheim wondered how everyone would respond."

Holmes turned to the shaken Durkheim.

"You did not anticipate, did you, that Professor Weber would strike you, that Lady Bracknell would faint and that her diamond would break loose from the chain to which it was attached?"

While Durkheim looked abashed, Holmes explained to the rest of us, "After reading the letter, I came to Claridge's to interview the rest of you. I wanted to know how many of you knew this was an experiment of Durkheim's. If anyone did know, he would have a good reason to further the experiment by stealing the diamond. After speaking to all of you, and examining the hotel, it became more clear that Durkheim had taken the jewel. The diamond rolled toward Durkheim, so he picked it up and left the room, saying that he would look for something to revive Lady Bracknell. When he saw the secluded ice room, he chipped some ice, laid the stone in the pile, and brought an ice pack to Lady Bracknell.

"His experiment progressed, then, from a simple provocation to an actual crime—albeit an odd crime. He could not resist, it seems, expanding his experiment and seeing how you, his colleagues, reacted. Yet, he was not at Claridge's to observe what happened. All of this in the name of science, mind you, which raises questions about what sociologists should be allowed to do in their experiments.

"After everyone had been questioned and the premises searched—the police did not notice the clear diamond resting amongst chips of ice—Professor Durkheim got some ice to reduce the swelling on his face, put the diamond underneath the ice, and walked out of the room, ready to do some research on religion and the lower classes in London. It was while doing this research on evangelical sects that he was robbed and his wallet was taken by two toughs, who took the money and threw his wallet in a gutter near the Thames. This led Inspector Lestrade to fear that he had been murdered and to have men looking for his body in the river. Professor Durkheim ended up sleeping the night in a hostel maintained by one of the evangelical sects here in London.

"When Professor Durkheim returned to the hotel this afternoon, I picked his pocket and found the diamond. He was clearly feeling that his experiment and his research were more successful than he could have possibly have imagined. Many of you, I'm sure, do not feel the same way."

"I'm shocked, Professor Durkheim," cried out Lady Bracknell, "that you could subject me to such anguish. I cried the whole night and feared I would never see that diamond, which my late husband gave me, again. It was the worst night I've had since my husband passed away."

"It was bad enough for you to provoke an argument with Professor Weber," added Beatrice Webb, "but to subject Lady Bracknell, who has done so much to alleviate the problems of the poor, to such anguish, because of your interest in experimenting with us, was simply unconscionable. I cannot help but notice, sir, that it was a woman who suffered most from your lamentable experiment." Mrs. Webb put her hand on Lady Bracknell's shoulder and glared at Durkheim.

Georg Simmel joined the tirade, "I can understand your desire do research on us, to as you put it, 'provide us with an experience of the real world to counter our theoretical proclivities.' Still, I must condemn your behavior. Human interactions are of great interest to me, as you know, but you do not have the right to subject people to harrowing experiences in the name of science. It is quite immoral and, let me suggest, unproductive, from a scientific point of view."

"I agree," said Du Bois. "And I speak as a man who has had my share of real-world experiences of an even more painful nature. People of my race know the real world, Professor Durkheim. We know what it is like to be rejected and constantly humiliated because of the color of our skin. Not all of us are captives of our book-lined studies, as you are, sir."

"I can only say that I am shocked," said Marianne Weber, "at the way you treated my husband and poor Lady Bracknell. Provoking him into an argument, considering that he is not well, was insensitive, and then taking Lady Bracknell's diamond, all for an experiment, was not only illegal but contemptible. I am deeply offended by your behavior."

Durkheim looked ashamed at the attacks of his colleagues; he took a small notebook from his jacket pocket and held it in front of him like a tiny scientific shield.

Max Weber walked quickly over to Durkheim.

"You put me through this terrible anguish as an experiment?" he asked in a low voice. "Have you no decency or respect for people? Do you think that just because you are a sociologist you can do whatever you want to people in the name of science? Don't you have any sense of ethics? Don't you have any feeling for the rights of individuals? Think of what you put us all through . . . my dear wife, poor Lady Bracknell, Georg Simmel, myself, and everyone else! You should confine your work to theoretical matters, I suggest." He had an angry look on his face.

"But, Max," pleaded Durkheim. "I'm terribly sorry that things turned out the way they did, believe me. I had no desire to cause you or anyone else pain, but like many experiments, this one somehow went awry. I just wanted . . ."

Before he could finish, Weber punched him again—this time on the other side of his face.

"Mon Dieu!" shouted Durkheim, whose nose started bleeding again. He took a handkerchief to catch the blood. Then, he paused for a moment . . . and suddenly started laughing.

"I've turned the other cheek," he said.

"What do you make of it?" I asked Freud, who was sipping champagne and puffing away on a big cigar. The quick turnaround of the case stunned me.

"Very interesting, Dr. Watson," said Freud, taking a puff on his cigar. "Very interesting."

glos**sary**

Alienation. Marx argued that bourgeois capitalist societies inevitably generated alienation, a sense of estrangement and separation that members of the proletariat—that is, workers—feel from their work, from themselves, and from others in their societies. Literally, the word means no (a-) ties or connections (liens).

Anomie. Literally speaking, anomie means no (a-) norms (nomos). It refers to societies in which the norms are weak or changing and individuals either don't know or don't feel bound to obey the strictures of the society.

Bureaucracy. Bureaucracies are characterized by having permanent and hierarchically organized staffs, areas of authority that are controlled by detailed and specific rules and regulations, and a means of dealing with individuals that is objective and impersonal. Max Weber argued that in modern societies, bureaucratic forms, the most rational form of organization, dominate all institutions.

Charisma. Max Weber's term for leaders who gain power due to the qualities of their personalities. Authority, for Weber, moves from traditional (kings) to charismatic (personalities) and finally to bureaucratic modes (bureaucrats).

Class. From a linguistic standpoint, a class is any group of things that has something in common. We often use it to refer to social classes, or, more literally, socioeconomic classes: groups of people who differ in terms of income and lifestyle. Marxist theorists argue that there is a ruling class that shapes the ideas of the proletariat, the working classes.

Collective Consciousness. Durkheim's notion of collective consciousness is that groups hold certain coherently connected ideas that function for them as worldviews. To understand a group, one must understand its consciousness.

Collective Representations. Durkheim used this concept to deal with the fact that people are both individuals, pursuing their own aims, and social animals, who are guided by the groups and societies in which they find themselves. Collective representations are, broadly speaking, texts that reflect the beliefs and ideals of groups and other collectivities.

Concept. We will understand concept to be a general idea or notion that explains or helps us understand some phenomenon or phenomena. Thus, for example, Freudian psychoanalytic theory makes use of a number of concepts: the ego, the id, the Oedipus Complex, and so on.

Culture. There are hundreds of different definitions of this term. Generally speaking, culture involves the transmission between generations of specific ideas, arts, customary beliefs, ways of living, behavior patterns, institutions, and values.

Defense Mechanisms. In psychoanalytic theory, defense mechanisms are methods used by the ego to defend itself against pressures from id or impulsive elements in the psyche and superego elements such as conscience and guilt. Some of the more common defense mechanisms are repression (barring unconscious instinctual wishes, memories, and so on from consciousness); regression (returning to earlier stages in one's development); ambivalence (a simultaneous feeling of love and hate for some person); and rationalization (offering excuses to justify one's actions).

Deviance. This concept refers to individuals and groups of people whose values, beliefs, behavior patterns, and the rules they follow, are different from (that is deviate from) those of most people in a given society.

Disfunctional (also Dysfunctional). In sociological thought, something is disfunctional if it contributes to the breakdown or destabilization of the entity in which it is found.

Dyad. Simmel's term for a relationship among two elements, as contrasted, for example, with *triads,* which have three elements in them. Dyad relationships tend to have an "all or nothing" characteristic.

Elective Affinity. Max Weber's notion that certain ideas that can be connected to one another tend to seek each other out at certain times and come together, with important historical consequences. The same applies for groups that seem to seek one another out.

Ethnocentrism. This refers to the notion that some members of some ethnic groups have that their ideas, their customs, their beliefs, and their way of life are better than those held by other ethnic groups.

False Consciousness. In Marxist thought, false consciousness refers to mistaken ideas that people have about their class, status, and economic possibilities. These ideas help maintain the status quo and are of great use to the ruling class, which wants to avoid radical changes in the social structure.

Feminism. Feminist critics attack the roles given to women in society and the way they are treated by men. Contemporary feminist critics argue that women are typically used as sexual objects and are portrayed stereotypically in mass-mediated culture and this has negative affects on both men and women. In addition, they are exploited in their jobs and held down by a "glass ceiling."

Functional Alternative. Something which is an alternative to something—that is, it takes the place of something else. For example, professional football can be seen as a functional alternative to religion.

Functionalism. In sociological thought, the term "functional" refers to the contribution an institution makes to the maintenance of society. Something is functional if it helps maintain the system in which it is found.

Gender. This term refers to the sexual category of an individual: masculine or feminine, and to behavioral traits connected with each category.

Hypothesis. A hypothesis is something that is assumed to be true for the purposes of discussion or argument or further investigation. It is, in a sense, a guess or supposition that is used to explain some phenomenon.

Ideal Type. Max Weber's notion that an imaginary and extreme example of something that does not exist but that can be useful as an analytical tool. Ideal types, Weber said, involve "one-sided exaggeration or accentuation of the elements of a phenomena" to make them more understandable and useful for theoretical purposes.

Ideology. An ideology refers to a logically coherent, integrated explanation of social, economic, and political matters that help establish the goals and direct the actions of some group or political entity.

Latent Functions. Latent functions are hidden, unrecognized, and unintended functions of some activity, entity, or institution. They are contrasted by social scientists with manifest functions, which are recognized and intended.

Lifestyles. This term which means, literally, style of life, refers to the way people live—to the decisions they make about how to decorate their apartments or homes (and where they are located), the kind of cars they drive, to the clothes they wear, to the kinds of foods they eat and the restaurants they frequent, to where they go for vacations, and so on.

Manifest Functions. The manifest functions of some activity, entity, or institution are those that are obvious and intended. Manifest functions contrast with latent functions, which are hidden and unintended.

Materialism. The notion that the social and economic conditions found in societies shapes consciousness, not ideas. As Marx explained, society determines consciousness, not consciousness society.

Mechanical Solidarity. Durkheim's term for societies in which "ideas and tendencies common to all members of the society are greater in number and intensity than those which pertain personally to each member." That is, individual differences tend to be minimized, unlike societies characterized by organic solidarity, where differences among individuals are of major importance. *See* organic solidarity.

Model. Models, in the social sciences, are abstract representations that show how some phenomenon functions. Theories are typically expressed in language but models tend to be represented graphically or by statistics or mathematics. Denis McQuail and Svend Windahl define "model" in *Communication Models for the Study of Mass Communication* (1993:2) as "a consciously simplified description in graphic form of a piece of reality. A model seeks to show the main elements of any structure or process and the relationships between these elements."

Nonfunctional. In sociological thought, something is nonfunctional if it is neither functional nor disfunctional, but plays no role in the entity in which it is found.

Organic Solidarity. Durkheim argued that in modern societies, ties between people aren't as strong or secure as in more primitive societies, characterized by mechanical solidarity. Organic solidarity is based on differences between people and is a product of the division of labor in modern, industrial societies.

Protestant Ethic. Max Weber argued that it was the Protestant ethic of "inner-world asceticism," which involved transferring religious principles and religious discipline from the inner to the outer world and glorifying the accumulation of wealth that was responsible for the rapid development of capitalism in the western world.

Psychoanalytic Theory. Psychoanalytic theory is based on the notion that the human psyche has what Freud called the "unconscious" which is inaccessible to us ordinarily speaking (unlike consciousness and the preconscious) and which continually shapes and affects our mental functioning and behavior. We can symbolize this by imagining an iceberg: the tip of the iceberg, showing above the water, represents consciousness. The part of the iceberg we can see, just below the surface of the water, represents the preconscious. And the rest of iceberg (most of it cannot be seen but we know it is there) represents the unconscious. We cannot access this area of our psyches because of repression. This is Freud's "topographic" hypothesis. Freud also emphasized matters such as sexuality and the role of the Oedipus Complex in everyone's lives. He also developed a "structural hypothesis," which divided the human psyche into three components: the id (the psychic representatives of human drives), the ego (that which helps individuals deal with their environment), and the superego (guilt, conscience, moral precepts).

Race. There is considerable disagreement about how to define race. Traditionally it has been defined as involving genetically inherited distinctive physical characteristics, but in recent years many social scientists have argued that race is socially constructed—that is, race is a culturally defined concept.

Relativism. In philosophical thought, relativism refers to the belief that truth is relative and not absolute; there are no objective standards. In ethical thought, relativism suggests there are no absolutes of morality and ethics. Thus, different societies have different ways of living and practices that are as valid as any others. That is, morality and ethical behavior are relative to particular groups and cannot be generalized to include all human beings. This contrasts with the notion that there are ethical absolutes or universals—which can and should be applied to everyone.

Role. A role is a way of behaving that we learn in society and that is appropriate to a particular situation. A person generally plays many roles during a given day: parent (family), worker (job), and so on.

Ruling Class. In Marxist theory, societies are divided into contending classes. The bourgeoisie is the ruling class whose ideas dominate the thinking of the working class, the proletariat.

Social Controls. Social controls are ideas, beliefs, values, and mores people get from their societies that shape their beliefs and behavior. People are both individuals, with certain distinctive physical and emotional characteristics and desires, and also, at the same time, members of societies. And people are shaped, to varying degrees, by the institutions found in these societies.

Social Facts. Durkheim defined a social fact as "every way of acting, fixed or not, capable of exercising on an individual an external constraint." These constraints become internalized in peoples' consciousness as moral guides and help shape their behavior.

Social Interaction. Sociologists argue that society can be defined as patterned interactions, which means sociology becomes the study of human interactions in various settings and situations.

Socialization. This term refers to the processes by which societies teach individuals how to behave: what rules to obey, roles to assume, and values to hold. Socialization was traditionally done by parents, by educators, by religious figures, and by peers. The mass media and popular culture seem to have usurped this function to a considerable degree nowadays, with consequences that are not always positive.

Sociation. Sociation refers to the ways in which people form groups and interact with one another. As Georg Simmel explained, "Sociology asks what happens to men and by what rules they behave, not insofar as they unfold their understandable individual existences in their totalities, but insofar as they form groups and are determined by their group existence because of interaction."

Sociological Theory. Sociological theories are systematic and logical attempts to explain and predict social behavior. Theories differ from concepts, which define certain phenomena that are being studied (for example, anomie), and from models, which are abstract, usually graphic in nature, and explicit about what is being studied. As we will understand the term, "sociological theory" refers to the ideas and explanations offered by sociologists about sociological phenomena—generally speaking, the behavior of people in groups. Sociological thought is not necessarily divorced from research, as Durkheim's study of suicide reveals.

Sociology. Sociology can be defined as the scientific study of human social life. It is a social science that attempts to describe, understand, and predict the behavior of human groups.

Stereotypes. Stereotypes are widely held, overly simple, and generally inaccurate group portraits of categories of people. These stereotypes can be positive, negative, or mixed, but generally they are negative in nature. Stereotyping always involves making gross overgeneralizations. (All Mexicans, Chinese, Jews, African Americans,

WASPs, Americans, lawyers, doctors, professors, etc. are held to have certain characteristics, usually something negative.)

Subculture. Subcultures are cultural subgroups whose religion, ethnicity, sexual orientation, beliefs, values, behaviors, lifestyles, and so on vary in certain ways from those of the dominant culture. In any complex society, it is normal to have a considerable number of subcultures.

Suicide. This term means, literally, murdering oneself (sui = oneself; side = killing). It refers to voluntarily and intentionally taking one's own life. Durkheim's research led him to suggest that there are a number of different kinds of suicide—egoistic, anomic, altruistic, and fatalistic suicide—and to connect rates of suicide to the amount of cohesiveness and integration existing in a given society.

Values. Values are abstract and general beliefs or judgments about what is right and wrong, what is good and bad. Values have implications for individual behavior and for social, cultural, and political entities. There are a number of problems with values from a philosophical point of view. First, how does one determine which values are correct or good and which aren't? That is, how do we justify values? Are values objective or subjective? Second, what happens when there is a conflict between groups, each of which holds central values that conflict with those of a different group?

biblio**graphy**

Adams, Bert N., and R. A. Sydie. *Sociological Theory.* Thousand
Oaks, Calif.: Pine Forge Press, 2001.

Berger, Arthur Asa. *Essentials of Mass Communication Theory.*
Thousand Oaks, Calif.: Sage, 1995.

———. *Postmortem for a Postmodernist.* Walnut Creek, Calif.: AltaMira
Press, 1997.

———. *The Mass Comm Murders: Five Media Theorists Self-Destruct.*
Lanham, Md.: Rowman & Littlefield, 2002.

Berger, Peter, and Brigitte Berger. *Sociology: A Biographical Approach.*
New York: Basic Books, 1972.

Burns, Elizabeth, and Tom Burns, eds. *Sociology of Literature and
Drama.* Baltimore: Penguin, 1973.

Chinoy, Ely. *Sociological Perspective.* 2d ed. New York: Random
House, 1968.

Coleman, James S., and Deepak Lai. *Foundations of Social Theory.*
Cambridge, Mass.: Harvard University Press, 1994.

Coser, Lewis A. *Masters of Sociological Thought: Ideas in Historical
and Social Context.* New York: Harcourt Brace Jovanovich, 1971.

Du Bois, W. E. B. *Black Folk, Then and Now.* Millwood, N.Y.: Kraus-
Thomson, 1975.

Durkheim, Emile. *Suicide: A Study in Sociology.* Translated by J. A. Spaulding and G. Simpson. New York: Free Press, 1952.

———. *Moral Education.* New York: Free Press, 1962.

———. *The Elementary Forms of the Religious Life.* New York: Free Press, 1965.

Freud, Sigmund. *Group Psychology and the Analysis of the Ego.* Translated by James Strache. New York: Boni and Liveright, 1921.

Frisby, David, and Mike Featherstone. *Simmel on Culture.* London: Sage, 1997.

Gerth, H. H., and C. Wright Mills. *From Max Weber: Essays in Sociology.* New York: Oxford University Press, 1946.

Hansen, Donald A. *An Invitation to Critical Sociology: Involvement, Criticism, Exploration.* New York: Free Press, 1976.

Hughes, H. Stuart. *Consciousness and Society: The Reorientation of European Social Thought 1890–1930.* New York: Vintage, 1958.

Jenks, Chris, ed. *Core Sociological Dichotomies.* London: Sage, 1998.

Larson, Calvin J. *Major Themes in Sociological Theory.* New York: David McKay, 1973.

Lenin, Vladimir. *State and Revolution.* New York: International, 1932.

———. *Imperialism: The Highest Stage of Capitalism.* New York: International, 1937.

Park, Peter. *Sociology Tomorrow: An Evaluation of Sociological Theories in Terms of Science.* New York: Pegasus, 1969.

Rickman, Jonathan, ed. *A General Selection from the Works of Sigmund Freud.* Garden City, N.Y.: Anchor, 1957.

Ritzer, George. *Sociological Theory.* New York: McGraw-Hill, 1995.

———. *Classic Sociological Theory.* New York: McGraw-Hill, 1999.

Ruitenbeek, Hendrik M., ed. *Varieties of Classic Social Theory.* New York: E. P. Dutton, 1963.

Shils, Edward, and Henry Finch, eds. *Max Weber on the Methodology of the Social Sciences.* New York: Free Press, 1949.

Simmel, Georg. "Adornment." In *The Sociology of Georg Simmel,* edited and translated by Kurt H. Wolff, 338–44. Glencoe, Ill.: Free Press, 1950.

———. "The Poor." Translated by Claire Jacobson. *Social Problems* 13, no. 2 (fall 1965): 118–39.

———. "Money in Modern Culture." *Theory, Culture & Society* 8, no. 3 (1991): 17–31.

Thompson, Kenneth, and Jeremy Tunstall, eds. *Sociological Perspectives.* Middlesex: Penguin Books, 1971.

Volosinov, V. N. *Freudianism: A Critical Sketch.* Translated by I. R. Titunik. Bloomington: Indiana University Press, 1987.

Webb, Beatrice. *The Diary of Beatrice Webb Volume 3 1905–1924: The Power to Alter Things.* London: Virago Press, 1984.

Weber, Max. *The Protestant Ethic and the Spirit of Capitalism.* Translated by Talcott Parsons. New York: Scribner's, 1958.

———. *Wirtschaft und Gesselschaft.* In *From Max Weber: Essays in Sociology,* edited and translated by H. H. Gerth and C. Wright Mills. New York: Oxford University Press, 1946.

Selected Works by the Theorists Depicted Herein

Du Bois, W. E. B. *The Souls of Black Folk.* Chicago: A. C. McLung, 1903.

———. *The Philadelphia Negro: A Social Study.* Philadelphia: University of Pennsylvania Press, 1998.

———. *John Brown.* New York: Modern Library, 2001.

Durkheim, Emile. *The Rules of Sociological Method.* New York: Free Press, 1938.

———. *Suicide.* Glencoe, Ill.: Free Press, 1961.

———. *The Elementary Forms of the Religious Life.* New York: Free Press, 1965.

Freud, Sigmund. *Totem and Taboo.* Translated by James Strachey. New York: W. W. Norton, 1913.

———. *Group Psychology and the Analysis of the Ego.* Translated by James Strachey. New York: Boni and Liveright, 1921.

———. *Civilization and Its Discontents.* Translated by J. T. Riviere. London: Hogarth Press, 1930.

Lenin, Vladimir. *State and Revolution.* New York: International, 1932.

———. *Imperialism: The Highest Stage of Capitalism.* New York: International, 1937.

———. *What Is to Be Done?* New York: International, 1939.

Simmel, Georg. *The Sociology of Georg Simmel.* Edited and translated by Kurt H. Wolff. New York: Free Press, 1950.

———. *Conflict and the Web of Group Affliliations.* Edited and translated by Kurt H. Wolff. New York: Free Press, 1965.

———. *Simmel on Culture.* Edited by David Frisby and Mike Featherstone. London: Sage, 1997.

Webb, Beatrice. *My Apprenticeship.* Cambridge, U.K.: Cambridge University Press, 1980.

———. *The Diary of Beatrice Webb Volume 3 1905–1924: The Power to Alter Things.* London: Virago Press, 1984.

———. *The Co-operative Movement in Great Britain.* London: Ashgate, 1987.

Weber, Max. *The Theory of Social and Economic Organization.* New York: Oxford University Press, 1947.

———. *The Methodology of the Social Sciences.* Glencoe, Ill.: Free Press, 1949.

———. *The Protestant Ethic and the Spirit of Capitalism.* Translated by Talcott Parsons. New York: Scribner's, 1958.

Index

about the **author**

ARTHUR ASA BERGER is professor of broadcast and electronic communication arts at San Francisco State University, where he has taught since 1965. He graduated in 1954 from the University of Massachusetts, where he majored in literature and philosophy. He received an M.A. degree in journalism and creative writing from the University of Iowa in 1956. He was drafted shortly after graduating from Iowa and served in the U.S. Army in the Military District of Washington in Washington, D.C., where he was a feature writer and speechwriter in the District's Public Information Office. He also wrote high school sports for *The Washington Post* on weekend evenings.

Berger spent a year touring Europe after he got out of the Army and then went to the University of Minnesota, where he received a Ph.D. in American studies in 1965. He wrote his dissertation on the comic strip *Li'l Abner.* In 1963–1964 he had a Fulbright to Italy and taught at the University of Milan. He spent a year as visiting professor at the Annenberg School for Communication at the University of Southern California, Los Angeles, in 1984. He also taught at Heinrich Heine University in Dusseldorf in the winter of 2001 as a Fulbright Senior Specialist.

He is the author of numerous articles, book reviews, and books on the mass media, popular culture, humor, and everyday life. Among his recent books are *Media Analysis Techniques, Media and Communication Research Methods, The Art of Comedy Writing,* and *Video Games: A Popular Culture Phenomenon.* His books have been translated into German, Swedish, Italian, Korean, Indonesian, and Chinese. He has lectured in more than a dozen countries in the course of his career.

Berger is married, has two children and one grandchild, and lives in Mill Valley, California. His wife teaches philosophy at Diablo Valley College. He enjoys travel and dining in ethnic restaurants.

He can be reached by e-mail at: aberger@sfsu.edu.